David Adam was born in Alnwick, Northumberland. He was Vicar of Danby on the North Yorkshire Moors for over 20 years, where he discovered the gift for writing prayers in the Celtic pattern. His first book of these, *The Edge of Glory*, achieved immediate popularity. He has since published several collections of prayers and meditations based on the Celtic tradition and the lives of the Celtic saints. His books have been translated into various languages, including Finnish and German, and have appeared in American editions. Many of his prayers have now been set to music. After thirteen years as Vicar of Holy Island, where he had taken many retreats and regularly taught school groups on prayer, David moved to Waren Mill in Northumberland from where he continues his work and writing.

# LIVING IN
# TWO KINGDOMS

DAVID ADAM

First published in Great Britain in 2007

Society for Promoting Christian Knowledge
36 Causton Street
London SW1P 4ST

*British Library Cataloguing-in-Publication Data*
A catalogue record for this book is available from the British Library

ISBN 978–0–281–05775–7

1 3 5 7 9 10 8 6 4 2

Typeset by Graphicraft Ltd, Hong Kong
Printed in Great Britain by CPI Bookmarque, Croydon, CR0 4TD

Produced on paper from sustainable forests

*No heaven can come to us unless our hearts find rest in
   it today.*
                    *Take heaven!*
*No peace lies in the future which is not hidden in the
   present.*
                    *Take peace!*
                              (Fra Giovanni, 1513)

# Contents

# Acknowledgements

The author and publisher acknowledge with thanks permission to reproduce extracts from the following:

Ifor Williams, *The Beginnings of Welsh Poetry*, p. 102, University of Wales Press, 1972.

'Walking Away' from *The Complete Poems* by C. Day Lewis, published by Sinclair-Stevenson, 1992. Copyright © 1992 in this edition The Estate of C. Day Lewis. Reprinted by permission of The Random House Group Ltd.

*The Book of a Thousand Prayers* by Angela Ashwin. Copyright © 1996. Used by permission of Zondervan.

*Enfolded in Love*, trans. by members of the Julian Shrine, 1980, copyright © Darton, Longman & Todd.

The Paschal Homily of St John Chrysostom, from Clément, Olivier (trans. Theodore Berkeley ocso), 1993, *The Roots of Christian Mysticism*, New City Press.

Every effort has been made to seek permission to use copyright material reproduced in this book. The publisher apologizes for those cases where permission might not have been sought and, if notified, will formally seek permission at the earliest opportunity.

# Introduction

Throughout my life there has been a slowly growing awareness of a greater depth and an abiding presence in this very extra-ordinary world of ours. There is no sudden illumination but rather points where a little more light is revealed. There are nudges in a certain direction rather than ever taking a sure path. Nothing is forced upon me but I am offered the choice of something more than a material world. While still striving for greater awareness, I am convinced that we all belong to more than the earth. Though this earth is a wonder-filled home there is more to life than just living on this planet. We belong to another kingdom, the kingdom of God. I avoid calling it the kingdom of heaven, for that implies for most people that it is far off. In fact the kingdom of heaven is at hand and we are invited to enjoy it every day. Our God is not one who made the world and then left it to its own devices but is deeply involved in it and ever present, waiting to be known and loved by us. This book seeks to be a journey taking us deeper into the kingdom of God.

Here are some words from Thomas Traherne: 'Your enjoy-ment of the world is never right, till every morning you awake in heaven; see yourself in your Father's Palace; and look upon the skies, the earth, and air as Celestial Joys; Having such an esteem among all as if you were among the Angels.'

Now there is a challenge. Do you see yourself in your 'Father's Palace'? Are you aware that you are in his kingdom?

## Introduction

Let us journey together into a deeper knowledge that we are living in two kingdoms.

Again Traherne says: 'You never enjoy the world aright, till you love the beauty of enjoying it, and that you are covetous and earnest to persuade others to enjoy it.'

This is meant to be a journey of delight, a pleasurable exploration into the wonders and mystery of the world and our own being. It is a journey of love: a journey with God and into God. The aim is to discover, in the words of Shakespeare from *Twelfth Night*, 'journeys end in lovers meeting'. Yet in another sense it is a journey without end, for it concerns eternal life and a relationship with God who is eternal.

I have always had a great love for the world. I was fortunate to come from a loving home. We did not have many resources but we did have love. We were often struggling against various difficulties but we had the support and care of each other. To be loved makes us see the world in a special way and for this I am thankful for a loving home. From an early age I learnt to treasure simple things and common objects. I had a love for the world that so willingly shared itself with me. I still thrill to know that 'God so loved the world' and that he sent his Son into the world and for love of the world. We are not only offered the love of God but we are also invited to love his creation as he loves it. To be a believer in a loving Creator is an invitation to enjoy and love life. The Christian faith in every way is life-expanding and not life-denying. To become a Christian is to enter into a greater world than many see and to have hope for the future as well as joy in the now.

As a youngster, I always wanted to know more. I liked to climb the next hill and see around the next corner. My mother said I always wanted to see the 'back of beyond'. I was never quite sure what she meant but I was often aware of a beyond or an otherness in the midst of what was obvious.

While still in the junior school I asked for two special gifts on separate occasions. I wanted a telescope to look at the moon and the stars and a microscope to look at things more closely. Pictures of snowflakes perfectly patterned each with their own individual shape amazed me. Because of the money spent on these, not a lot, neither the telescope nor the microscope was much improvement on my natural sight. The important thing was that they helped me to focus. I spent hours looking at the moon and stars in wonder. On clear winter nights I enjoyed being out wrapped up against the cold and enraptured by what I saw. Instead of gazing at them all I concentrated on a little area at a time. It was the same with the microscope. I spent ages focusing on a beetle, a leaf or a small flower, though I must admit I could never get a snowflake under the microscope without it disappearing before I could fully focus. I was learning to look long and closely at things, I was learning to focus: to give my undivided attention to something. Instead of it just being an object it became a subject in its own right and had something to show me or teach me. Sadly the art of giving one's undivided attention to anything for long is one that we are in danger of losing in a world of speed and multi-choice. We all need time for contemplation, for being still with the 'temple' of the world and letting it draw us into deeper depths. You may like to call this 'keeping focused'.

To keep me occupied as an active junior, I was sent to the local cinema two or three times every week. Story and adventure were things I looked forward to seeing. I saw that life was bigger than what was around me and that often it was a struggle. In the days of my growing up nearly all films were still about good triumphing over evil and had happy endings. It would be only much later that I realized that many stories were biased in favour of the conquerors, as is the writing of history. At this stage I was not aware how often behind nice films was a story of oppression and of land grabbing. I now shudder to see how people are robbed of their heritage in the name of progress or by a greater power. One of my favourite proverbs from Africa says: 'Until lions have their own storytellers, tales of the lion hunt will always glorify the hunter.' But this was the days when most films were in black and white with black-and-white thinking. Yet the cinema opened up visions of other people and different ways of living.

I was fascinated by stories of other worlds and other lives. I noticed how good usually triumphed in the end. I also saw how the greedy and the grasping caused trouble for themselves and for others. In the stories about discovering new worlds I was fascinated to discover how they were often within this world and could be come across by accident or by a searching that demanded that other things did not put the seeker off, no matter how costly or dangerous. This was just the same as the folk tales I liked reading; many of these were sure there was another world woven into ours and just waiting to be discovered. I love the world I live in but I always have a feeling that there is much more to our world than this; the world is far bigger, more wonderful and more mysterious than we can see even in our dreams. Instead of 'another world' I became fascinated by this world and its otherness. The world is far deeper than any of us have fathomed. Later I would discover not only the otherness of the world but the great Other who is within it. I do not seek other worlds. I seek to know the world of the other and to share in it.

My aunt took me to see a film with Mario Lanza in it and he sang,

> I'll walk with God from this day on,
> His guiding hand will lead me on.

I cannot now remember much about this film but I was amazed at the idea that you could walk with God. This was one of those moments of illumination. Fortunately, my Aunt Connie bought a 78 rpm recording for her gramophone so I heard it again and again. For me the action of walking with God was mind-boggling, and it still is. To discover that God is not far off and that prayer is not a long-distance phone call is something that calls us to react to it. Only later would I discover in Celtic prayers an expression of joy in walking with God. I would also meet people who walked and talked with God in a most natural way and not just in church or in the words of the Church. God and his kingdom are not far off; they are at hand and waiting for us to come to them. I was slowly learning that Christianity was not a set of dogmas but rather about a relationship with the living God.

The idea of walking with God was strengthened by an experience I had soon after when I joined the church choir. I only did it because a friend went – or so I thought. It was the week before the Fourth Sunday in Advent, the Sunday before Christmas. The choir rehearsal was at 6.30 p.m. I walked through a cold dark churchyard full of headstones in fear and trembling. A lively imagination can often be a bother! The choir stalls were in a pool of light within a dim church, almost as far away from the door as possible. There was a feeling of moving towards the light and safety. We would spend the evening rehearsing carols but first there was an anthem to be sung for the Sunday. The words were taken from the first reading for that Sunday, 'Rejoice in the Lord alway, and again I say, Rejoice' (Philippians 4.4, BCP). The choirmaster made us sing this over and over. At one stage he came over to me while the singing was going on and said, 'Rejoice, boy! Let me see you smile when you sing this. Show that you are glad that God is here!' I found it hard to smile and look at the words and to sing but the words of the anthem became the first words of Scripture I learnt by heart. Not only were they committed to memory but into the heart. Singing over and over 'Rejoice in the Lord', 'the Lord is at hand' and 'be careful for nothing' in worship helped the reality to enter deeper into my being. Not only to acknowledge a presence and rejoice in it but to smile because of it. Perhaps that is what Psalm 43 in the Book of Common Prayer means when it says: 'O put thy trust in God: for I will yet give him thanks, which is the help of my countenance and my God.' Can trust in God affect not only the way you look at the world but also the way you look? Sometimes a good simple exercise is to follow the advice of my choirmaster: 'Smile, for God is here.'

That night, after the rehearsal, I could not sleep for thinking upon the words of the anthem and hearing them again and again in my mind. Years later, I would be greatly interested in 'recital theology', that is songs, hymns and rhythmical prayers that help to deepen our awareness and give us words to help us express what is in fact almost inexpressible. Prayers and hymns that have a rhythm or a beat are more easily remembered and not only help us to say something about our feelings and awareness but also deepen them. There is something about letting the words vibrate not only on our lips but also in our hearts and lives that deepens their impact. Later, just a snatch of a tune can bring back the memory of the words, the feelings and the occasion. Though some have compared this with positive thinking, I want to say it is much more than that. Some forms of positive thinking can be positively stupid! Recital theology and affirming the presence of God are to do with reality and opening our whole being to that reality. Positive thinking sets out to make a series of events happen; affirmation and recital theology seek to tune to what is actually real and happening.

Though understanding what was going on in church was still very much beyond me, the local vicar invited me to help him on Sundays and at Wednesday morning Communion services. Whether he saw some potential in me or just needed an extra helper I do not know, but the devotion of this man had a lasting influence on me. He explained to me that I was to serve and that meant giving him the bread and the wine for Communion and pouring water over his hands in a washing. Easy! But he then talked to me about the sanctuary and told me I had to respect it as a special holy place. 'You should never just walk into the sanctuary without pausing and reminding yourself you are in the Presence and approaching God. Even in a church the sanctuary is a special holy place.' This was not only news; it had a wonderful air of mystery and privilege. I am still only beginning to understand this but I know having special holy places is important. If we do not have a special holy place it is likely we have nowhere at all. At some stage it is important to discover our own holy places. As if to hammer this home, I was then told before I entered the sanctuary for the Communion service there were special prayers to say. I was given these on a little printed card. It was relatively simple, Psalm 43 to say and a confession to make of our unworthiness, opening us up to the love and forgiveness of God. We recited alternate verses of the psalm and I loved saying, 'that I may go unto the altar of God, even unto the God of my joy and gladness'. When all was done we had a short silence and only then entered the sanctuary. This learning to pause and to wait in the Presence is something I am still learning. I always try to have this pause and stillness whenever I enter a place that is called holy. Sadly today we find it hard to stop and be still. In our culture of speed and multi-choice we

difficult to pause: we have to be forever doing something
a.    moving on.

> There was always more
> In the world
> Than man could see,
> Walked they ever so slowly . . .
> they will see it no better
> for going fast.
>     (John Ruskin, 1819–1900)

It would do us all good to take to heart the words, 'Be still, and
know that I am God!' (Psalm 46.10).

There is a lovely story about a group of Europeans in the jungle. The Europeans were so anxious to get ahead in the jungle.
They wanted to cover as much ground as possible. They moved
on and on. Finally in a clearing the porters refused to go any
further. The leader explained, 'We are not moving.' When asked
why, he replied, 'We have come so far and so fast that we need
to stop. We have to wait for our souls to catch up with us.' Is
there not a danger for us in all noise, busyness and the speed at
which we are able to do things that we 'leave our souls behind'?
We are so occupied by the world and its demands that we fail to
enter into the other kingdom that is there and being offered
to us. In the clamour of the world it is difficult to pause and
enter the Presence and peace that is offered to us. It is of utmost
importance to find a holy resting place, for such a place is often
the door into the greater world where the two kingdoms
become one.

I was fortunate. At the stage of needing to learn silence I was
literally plunged into it. I went to work in a coal mine. I left
school at 15 to 'earn a living'. After school, I delighted in the
freedom and camaraderie of the new friends that I worked

with. As ever, money brought new freedoms and options; life was expanding rapidly. But the strange gift of the coal mine was a profound silence. After training I was asked to work on my own looking after a conveyor belt filling pit tubs with coal. There was the constant sound of machinery and coal tumbling into tubs but I worked alone for seven hours a day, only occasionally seeing someone or being telephoned to stop or start machinery. A friend, in a similar job further along the same conveyor belt system, would ring me to play me a new tune he had learnt on the mouth organ! But the two impressions I am still left with are the total darkness if the light you are wearing goes out and the silence – a silence that was almost tangible – when the machinery was switched off. I was given time to think, to be aware of my surroundings and of my own feelings. I was able to focus and look long and hard at what was around me. I was suddenly aware that I was working in what had been a forest about 300 million years ago and now was fossilized as coal. Above my head, girders held up a stone roof that was made up of thousands of fossilized shells and simple sea creatures. Once, many millennia before my time, this had been the seabed of a shallow sea that teemed with life. Above that were layers and layers of earth that reflected many stages in the formation of the world and with the right knowledge could be read like a book. Over and over these thoughts filled me with awe and showed me in a way how small we are in the ordering of the world. I had no doubt that it is an ordered world and that we who are here now have taken a long time in our making. It was a humbling experience and yet it opened up many avenues. I was being nudged again.

To leave the darkness of the coal mine after working through the night and to enter the light of a spring morning or a summer's day was another eye-opener. It was great to rejoice in the light and in the colour and beauty of the world. A poem by

Emily Dickinson expresses how I felt then, and still do, about the world.

> But were it told me – Today –
> That I might have the sky
> For mine – I tell you that my Heart
> Would split, for size of me –
>
> The Meadows – mine –
> The Mountains – mine –
> All Forests – Stintless Stars –
> As much of Noon as I could take
> Between my finite eyes –
>
> The Motion of the Dipping Birds –
> The Morning's Amber Road –
> For Mine – to look at when I liked –
> The News would strike me dead.
>              (Emily Dickinson, 1830–86)

This was not a desire to possess but rather to acknowledge the joy of being given these great gifts and to be part of a wonderful world. It was a delight to rejoice in each day, in the light, and in the beauty around me. I was and am very much at home in the world. Every day presented me with new things to wonder at and celebrate. I did not need another world, for this was a wonder-filled world that God had given to me. After working the night hours underground, I felt it was necessary to have something of the light and glory of the day and to rejoice in it rather than just close my eyes and sleep.

One day a friend and I went bird-nesting, not to take eggs but to enjoy the search and the wonder of the variously shaped nests, eggs and chicks. Afterwards I came home and heard a Thomas Hardy poem called 'Proud Songsters' on the radio that gave me yet another nudge.

> The thrushes sing as the sun is going,
> The finches whistle in ones and pairs,
> And as it gets dark loud nightingales
> In bushes
> Pipe, as they can when April wears,
> As if all Time was theirs.
> These are brand-new birds of twelve-months' growing,
> Which a year ago, or less than twain,
> No finches were, no nightingales,
> Nor thrushes,
> But only particles of grain,
> And earth and air and rain.
>
> (Thomas Hardy, 1840–1928)

If you think about that you can only be filled with awe. I thrilled at finding eggs in nests, at seeing new birds and hearing birdsong, and I still do. In every egg is the mystery of life and creation. What a wonderful world!

In the same way, when I read about how the universe came into being and how apparently unique our world is I am filled with awe. I agree with Richard Dawkins in his book *Unweaving the Rainbow* when he says, 'The feeling of awed wonder that science can give us is one of the highest experiences of which the human psyche is capable. It is a deep aesthetic passion to rank with the finest that music can offer.'

Though agreeing with Dawkins on this level I cannot agree with him in the way he looks at religion and God. I would have thought such an expansive view of creation would have been brought to bear on the way he looked at his faith. Our faith is not separate from our experience but is meant to feed it and be fed by it. Even while very much in the dark and underground, I was faced with wonder upon wonder that was nudging me to a deeper awareness of God.

The world was very much a place where I felt at home and I wanted no other! Yet this visible world was interwoven with another strand I was only becoming aware of. I do not want to call it another world or even another kingdom, for that implies separation and is in danger of dualism. Heaven and earth are one: God's rule of love, the kingdom of God, is here and now in the world in which we live.

Here words fail me and I want to say with the fourth-century Welsh writer:

> The world cannot comprehend in song bright and
>     melodious,
> Even though the grass and trees could sing,
> All your wonders, O true Lord!
> The Father created the world by a miracle;
> It is difficult to express its measure.
> Letters cannot contain it, letters cannot comprehend it.
> > (Williams, 1972, p. 102)

Yet what letters cannot tell and what the mind can hardly grasp we can know in our heart. The world of the kingdom of God is part and parcel of this world. In reality it is better to say that this world in which we live is part of God's kingdom. As people of this world we are also children of God, live in his presence and can experience his love. The material and the spiritual are woven finely together in a way that makes them inseparable. The visible world of matter and the invisible world of spirit are not two worlds but one. We belong to both, here and now. For ease I will say we are people of two realms or two kingdoms.

But I do not want to imply separation – rather an interplay of the two that is vital to our well-being. This is not to deny a life beyond this world, beyond what we call death. But if life is eternal we are already in it! Eternity does not come after death, though clearer vision and a fuller life may. If there is eternal life, it has begun; we have it now. What are you doing with it? We should not put off for eternity that which we are given here and now. Perhaps rather than juggle with the idea of two kingdoms you should seek to live in the eternal now. Make yourself at home in the world and at home with God.

The nearness of the kingdom of God is central to the teaching of Jesus. It involves us in an understanding of himself, his world-view and his work. At the very beginning of St Mark's Gospel we get a summary of the good news: 'The time is fulfilled, and the kingdom of God has come near; repent and believe in the good news' (Mark 1.15). The good news is that God is at work in his world and his kingdom is here for us to take part in. The word Jesus uses for 'kingdom' means God's sovereignty over his people and the world that he has made. This is not the rule of a despot but that of a loving and caring father. The alternative use in Matthew of 'the kingdom of heaven' means the same thing as 'the kingdom of God'. Matthew is using the Jewish convention of talking about God without using his name, in case we take God's name in vain. The kingdom is a gift from God; it is not something we can create. It is not some Utopia to strive after; rather it is something we can accept and enjoy. It is not a disposition of the heart, the will or the mind, for it exists without us: it is of God. But it is there for any who seek to enter into it. I have always enjoyed the reply of the woman from County Kerry who was asked, 'Where is heaven?' Her reply was, 'About one-foot-six above us.' Heaven is that close, if not closer! All we have to do is stretch ourselves and we can enter into it. Heaven is not far away but close at hand.

God seeks a relationship with us and wants us to be part of his kingdom here and now.

Within the halls of debate there is always an argument about whether the kingdom is here and now, called realized eschatology; or whether it is only in the future, which is futuristic eschatology. When I listen to the debates I want to answer the question, 'Is it one or the other?' by a single word: 'Yes'. To opt for the present alone or the future alone is not enough. We are talking about God's reign, God's kingdom. It is here and now, though in a way not yet in its fullest sense. It is wherever God's will is done, wherever God and his love are revealed. So for you it can be now, though being the humans we are, it is not yet fully realized. The joy of this is that you can always move towards a greater awareness, a deeper realization and a closer relationship with God and his kingdom.

In St John's Gospel there is little mention of the kingdom. There is only a mention of it when Jesus speaks to the Pharisee Nicodemus (John 3.3, 5). In John's Gospel the term used for entering into God's kingdom is 'life' and used in the particular sense of meaning 'life in its fullness'. Jesus says how he comes that we may 'have life, and have it abundantly' (John 10.10). Irenaeus captures this idea when he says: 'The glory of God is a human being fully alive.'

I do not like to talk of everlasting life but rather of eternal life. For some the idea of everlasting life can only be everlastingly dull! Eternal life is not about duration but about a quality of life, about life in a certain relationship. There is only one who can be called truly eternal and that is God. Eternal life as we know it is living God's life, dwelling in him and knowing he is in us. It is a rising above the merely human, that which is passing away, and entering in to that which is of God. We do this when we learn of the love of God and to give our love to

God. The joy is that we can do this through the wonderful world in which we live.

This book is an exploration of coterminous living in the two kingdoms and enjoying both. In time one kingdom may decrease and fade for us but the other kingdom will continue as we enter a deeper awareness of God. Again and again we need to rejoice in the reality that the kingdom of heaven is at hand and offered to us now. To project the kingdom of God beyond this world is to deny ourselves the heritage that is ours.

Though I do not think history really repeats itself, I agree with the statement concerning Miss Garnet in *Miss Garnet's Angel*: 'Long ago she had decided that history does not repeat itself; but perhaps when a thing was true it went on returning in different likenesses, borrowing from what went before, finding new ways to declare itself' (Vickers, 2000, p. 330).

For this reason I believe the Scriptures have much to say to us. The realities they speak about are still the realities that we experience. The realities of our place in and our relationship with the world are much the same as those of our forebears on the deepest levels. Our attitudes to God and our use of our God-given freedom all remain much the same. What happens within the Bible stories often well illustrates what is happening to us today. There is a lovely story out of Tanzania about a woman who was asked why she always carried the Bible around and not any other books. She replied, 'You can always read books, only the Bible reads us.' There is a way in which the Bible is a story of our life and our relationship with God.

As a basis for this book I want to look at a story Jesus told in Luke 15.11–32. It is usually called 'the story of the Prodigal Son'. Although it has a single main point, the love of God, I want to look at it bit by bit, for it shows us how we react as humans and some of the issues we all have to face. The shortest summary I have heard of this parable is:

At home,
Sick of home,
Away from home,
Home sick,
Home.
(perhaps needing to add 'Not at home at home'!)

At this stage, I believe it would be well worth you reading through the story of the Prodigal Son from Luke 15 and seeing where it relates, if anywhere, to your life. Do not miss the reaction of the son who did not leave home, for he reflects the position of many of us who are not at home at home and not quite at home with ourselves or the world.

At the end of each chapter there are 'Exercises' to put into practice what has been said. There is an opportunity to enter into a time of quiet and to look at one of the parables of the kingdom as told by Jesus. The '5P Exercise' is offered as a good exercise for beginners and for all who want to think more deeply about the Scriptures. I have called it the '5P Exercise' for each part can be described by a word beginning with the letter 'P':

**Pause, Presence, Picture, Ponder, Promise**

This is a good way of letting the Scriptures or life be known to us in a deeper way. One of the parables of the kingdom is looked at this way at the end of each chapter. Because God is the creator of the world of nature and of grace, it is possible to see images of God at work through his world. In fact God speaks to us through his world, through our senses and through the material things around us. Each parable has a single point to make, though often it contains other pointers to look at. The parables of the kingdom seek to make us aware of God at work in his world and in us.

Each group of exercises will contain thoughts to ponder and will be rounded off with a prayer, which it would be good to learn. The following prayer by St Benedict (480–543) is one you may like to learn by using it regularly in your worship of the ever-present God.

> O gracious and holy Father,
> give us wisdom to perceive you,
> intelligence to understand you,
> diligence to seek you,
> patience to wait for you,
> eyes to behold you,
> a heart to meditate upon you,
> a life to proclaim you,
> through the power of the Spirit of our Lord Jesus Christ.
> Amen.

# At Home

The group of town children from the English–Scottish borders enjoyed themselves on the Holy Island of Lindisfarne. Though they were in strange surroundings they quickly made themselves at home. They had been on the beach seeking for treasure. Some had gone on 'safari' in the rock pools to see what they could catch or just enjoy. Another group was asked to bring something interesting back from the beach to show us. Part of the time, they had learnt to focus on objects by looking through a cardboard tube and keeping it trained on one object. Stories about the saints and local heroes moved their imagination. They had sung songs as well as creating some beautiful artwork and prayers. The sun had shone and the scenery was beautiful. Now it was time to leave. Before their departure the teacher sought a response from her class. She was hoping they would express some gratitude for what they had been given. 'It was guid, Miss,' said the first. The second repeated the same sentence and so did the third, 'It was guid, Miss.' The fourth felt she wanted to say more and she emphatically proclaimed in a loud voice, 'It was verra guid, Miss.' The children all laughed and clapped their hands. There was no doubt that they had enjoyed the day and delighted in it.

As I listened to them saying 'It was guid', it sounded like God looking at his creation and seeing after each day, 'It was good' and on the sixth day he 'saw . . . that . . . it was very good'

(Genesis 1.4, 12, 18, 21, 25, 31). We need to learn that, as the children delighted in their day, God delights in his creation. To say God saw that it was good is not a judgement between good and evil but rather an expression of joy. God rejoiced, delighted in his creation and God still continues to take pleasure in his creation. We are called to share in that delight, to learn to love the world with the great love that God has for the world. This is not to deny evil but it is to focus on the reality that the world belongs to God and it is basically good. Too much of life today is concentrated on evil and disasters, and people find it very hard to enjoy what is around them. We need to learn to delight in what we are given through the goodness of God. Jewish rabbis have a saying about the day of judgement: they tell us, on Judgement Day we will be met by Moses or God Almighty and simply asked, 'Did you enjoy the world God gave to you?' Now there is a wonderful question. Are you into enjoying the world?

The first story in the Bible tells us of God's delight in creation. Creation was not anything God had to do; it was out of love and for joy that he created the world. All that exists comes from God; there is nothing in the universe that has its being without the Creator. Throughout Genesis 1 we hear of God delighting in his creation; He is pleased with it and it is joy to Him. The telling of the creation story is like sharing in a great liturgy; one by one each part of the universe is brought into view as created by God and every time the response is 'and he was very pleased'. God did not create the world to despise it or forsake it but to delight in it and to love it. God created the world out of his joy and for joy.

I have always been worried about Christians who give the impression that the world is not a suitable place for them to live in and should not be enjoyed. I have never felt like singing, 'This world is not my home' nor 'There is a happy land far, far away'. I know both these songs have a truth to tell but to me they sound too denying of the world. This is the world that God has given us to live in. This is the life that God has given to us. How can we ask for another or seek another if we have not tried to appreciate the great gift we have been given? We need to learn to be at home in the world we have been given and to know that God is here. We need to be at home with God and know that even now we are offered his kingdom. The kingdom of God is at hand and we are invited to enter into it. We may want to say we are only, at best, on the frontiers of the kingdom but let us at least acknowledge we can make our home in it. Our journey is not just a linear travelling but is a travelling deeper into what is around us. This journey is about the heights we can rise to as much as distance covered. It is about a homecoming and a realization that we are able to be at home with God every moment.

God comes to us and speaks to us through the world, and we need to train our ears to hear, our eyes to see and our hearts to love. Too often we are in the present with divided attention. We need to focus our attention and not get distracted by too many things. Once something demands our attention we are faced with it and not just what we have heard about it. It is there in reality as a subject in its own right. Sometimes if we give it time and opportunity it will then reveal a depth to it we have not dreamed of. Wordsworth knew this experience and speaks of:

> ... objects recognised,
> In flashes, and with glory not their own.
> (William Wordsworth, 1770–1850)

A good beginning is to choose something new each day to admire and to wonder at. Too often we have not looked deeply enough or long enough into what is around us and we fail to appreciate what we have.

We are too ready to move on before we have enjoyed or understood what is offered to us. We need to learn to stop and discover the wonders around us. If we do not appreciate the world, I am not sure we can appreciate the Creator. If we are hardly aware of the visible things around us it is not likely we can enjoy the invisible. The kingdom of God is at hand but most of us are too busy to take notice or to enter it and enjoy it. Though the kingdom of God can be said to be 'the rule of God' we have to realize that this is a rule of love and not of law. God's kingdom is a free gift of grace but if we do not take time to accept it and unwrap it we will never fully enjoy it. God wants us to be at home with him in his world and that is here and now.

Every now and then I like to look at one of the wonderful images of the world that were taken from the moon. We live on a beautiful planet and as yet there is nothing like it in the universe. Our world is unique and so is the life upon it and that includes you. I look at the pictures of the world from space and read the 'circular' poem opposite.

Learn to be at home in the world and to marvel at it. Seek to love it and defend it and know that you would not exist without it. One of my favourite translations by Kuno Meyer of a prayer attributed to St Patrick is called 'The Deer's Cry'. I rejoice in its idea of a daily resurrection, something I will come back to later. After attributing his resurrection to the Holy Trinity, the saving acts of Christ, angels and archangels and all the saints, St Patrick turns to the world and says:

> I arise today
> Through the strength of heaven:
> Light of sun,

If the earth were only
a few feet in diameter, floating a
few feet above a field somewhere, people
would come from everywhere to marvel at it.
People would walk around it, marvelling at its big
pools of water, its little pools, and the water flowing
between the pools. People would marvel at the bumps
on it, and the holes in it, and they would marvel at the very
thin layer of gas surrounding it and the water suspended
in the gas. The people would marvel at the creatures
walking around the surface of the ball, and the creatures
in the water. The people would declare it as sacred
because it was the only one, and they would protect it so
that it would not be hurt. The ball would be the greatest
wonder known, and people would come to be healed, to
gain knowledge, to know beauty and to wonder how it
could be. People would come to love it and defend
it with their lives, because they would somehow know that their own lives, their own
roundness, could be nothing without
it. If the earth were only a few
feet in diameter.

(Source unknown)

Radiance of moon,
Splendour of fire,
Speed of lightning,
Swiftness of wind,
Depth of sea,
Stability of earth,
Firmness of rock.

(Meyer, pp. 25–6)

Not only does Patrick acknowledge his total dependence on God but on the earth itself. Without the light of the sun, the air we breathe, the cycle of water to refresh the earth, none of us would be here on this planet. God has made us one with the earth and dependent on it for this the home he has given to us. This world is our home and we need to cherish it. Yet at the same time it is full of the presence of God. According to tradition, when St Patrick met with the princess daughters of the pagan king Laoghaire they asked, 'Who is God? Of who is God and where is his dwelling?' The reply was a creation-centred credo:

> Our God is a God of all,
> The God of heaven and earth,
> Of seas and of the rivers;
> The God of the sun, and of the moon and of all the
>     stars:
> The God of the lofty mountains
> And the lowly valleys.
> He has his dwelling around heaven and earth,
> And sea and all that in them is.
> He inspires all,
> He gives life to all,
> He dominates all,
> He supports all.
> He lights the light of the sun.
> He furnishes the light of the night.
> He has made springs in dry land . . .
> He is God of heaven and earth . . .
> The God above heaven,
> And in heaven and under heaven.

For Patrick there was an awareness that it is through the earth and all of creation that God gives us his life and love. Given the opportunity the earth reveals God's presence, his glory, for 'earth is crammed with heaven'.

> Earth's crammed with heaven
> And every common bush afire with God,
> But only he who sees, takes off his shoes;
> The rest sit round it, and pluck blackberries,
> And daub their natural faces, unaware,
> More and more, from the first similitude.
> > (Elizabeth Barrett Browning, 1808–61,
> > from *Aurora Leigh*, Book vii)

'Every . . . bush afire with God'; but Moses had to find a particular bush that was ablaze before he could become aware that God was with him always. Jacob needed the experience of the night alone under the stars and the vision of angels to know that God is with him. Isaiah needed to have the experience of the death of the king and the empty throne being filled with the presence of the Holy One. Martin of Tours met God in a beggar. St Francis held him close in a leper. Each had to find this holy place or holy person before he could begin to discover that all is holy for all belongs to God. In *Le Milieu Divin*, Teilhard de Chardin says that God:

> is not far away from us, altogether apart from the world we see, touch, hear, smell and taste about us. Rather he awaits us at every instant of our action, in the work of the moment. There is a sense in which he is at the tip of my pen, my spade, my brush, my needle – of my heart and my thought . . . by virtue of Creation and still more

7

of Incarnation, *nothing* here below is *profane* for those who know how to see. On the contrary everything is sacred.

Are you aware of the sacredness of all of life, of the earth and of all creatures? Many of the present problems we face with the planet and its ecological balance, with the destruction of rain forests and the using up of so many of the earth's resources, would be nearer to a resolution if we had not put the sacred as something apart from the world in which we live. We would all tread the earth more gently if we accepted it is God's gift to us and that he is found within it.

One of the things I looked for with some groups on Holy Island was the protecting boundary around the Celtic monastic settlement. There was a similar boundary around the monastic cell on the tiny Cuthbert's Island. It is thought that this protective barrier was not more than two or three feet high. It would not keep anything out and it would only keep within it whatever or whoever chose to stay within. Inside the area were not only the church and the monastic dwellings but also most of their workplaces. The scriptorium for producing manuscripts, the bakery for food and the brewery for ale, the refectory and the blacksmith's were all within the monastic bounds. Many would spend most of their life within this circle both waking and sleeping. What did it signify? For it was not protection against raiders, as the Vikings would prove. It was an attempt to create 'sacred space'. Not that the rest did not belong to God but within all were expected to live by the rules of the kingdom of God and show the love of God. Within was an attempt to live out 'your kingdom come, your will be done, on earth as it is in heaven'. To put it in another way, here the presence of God was acknowledged, people were at home with

God and he with them. Here they sought a living and loving relationship with their Maker and with each other. This was something they chose to do in response to knowing they were God's people. They did not always succeed in their ideals but they did make it their aim. When they left to go out in mission they were seen as people of God, not only by their words but also by their deeds.

To create 'sacred space' is necessary for us all, for unless we have a sacred place it is likely nowhere will be sacred. Once we have a truly sacred space then slowly, for us, all places become sacred. Once we are truly at home with God in one place, we discover that God is with us and at home with us wherever we travel. The sacred space enclosure does not enable us to escape from the world God made but rather to enter deeper into it. It is in this space that we can enter into a deeper reality that the busy world often loses sight of. Here we show we are at home with God and that we love him.

In the fourth century AD Christian men and women left cities to go and live in the desert. There are many reasons why they did this but they can be summed up in two statements, 'to answer the call of the love of God' and 'to seek to live in God's kingdom'. They were men and women who did not want to be passively ruled and guided by a society that was decadent. They wanted to avoid the triviality of so much of life and live in the depths of awareness and their being. They saw a world that was not at home with God even when it had become officially 'Christian'. As ever the people of the world were in danger of giving little acknowledgement to God or his kingdom even when both were at hand. The Desert Fathers and Mothers sought to live in awareness of God and his love. They sought to live in a way that reflected the Presence. They would not have survived for long in the desert unless they were at home with God and aware of his love. They were not escaping from the world, none of us can, but seeking to know it as it truly is, interfused with the divine. By freeing themselves from so many things they could focus on what mattered to them. They witnessed to the fact that here on this earth is the beginning, for us, of God's kingdom. Most of them would not have survived in the desert and doing without many things unless they did it out of love. Above all they were witnessing that in this world they wanted to be with their beloved God, without too many interruptions. The desert may not attract us, for many of us it would not be a practical option, but we can all create space in our days to make sure we have time to be at home with God. If we are to enjoy the world aright we need to be able to focus our attention on the fact that it is more than the visible and more than the temporal. Only when we are at home with God can we truly enjoy the world we live in.

There has been a tendency to describe creation as *ex nihilo*, as 'out of nothing', but I cannot go along with that as a major statement. If you are created out of nothing it is to nothing that you will return. I know it is intended to emphasize the power of God and that he alone is the Creator, but there is a more important fact to learn first. Likewise if you say you are created 'out of dust and to dust you will return', you may be stating a physical fact but it tells us nothing of the hope of the resurrection and fails to recognize you are also a spiritual being. It is far more important to learn that you are created out of God, out of his own being, out of the love and the delight of God, and that it is to God's love and delight that you will return. You need to know that you come from God, belong to God and will return to God: to know that you are in God and God is in you.

I am fascinated by the 'Big Bang' theory of creation. Before the Big Bang there was nothing: no time, no space, only emptiness. Then in the first three minutes according to the 'inflation theory' the universe doubled in size every one million, million, million, million, millionths of a second. Ninety-eight per cent of all that exists in the universe was created in the first 180 seconds. In a sense all that makes your human body was there at the beginning in that sudden expansion on an incredible scale. At one stage in the growth of the universe you were part of an exploding star! For the moment I am content with this scientific theory of creation and enjoy it, but I am also content with the belief that says it was an explosion of love. God created the world out of his love and for his love. In a sense it is just as much an act of faith to accept the ungraspable and extraordinary numbers that science uses about creation, as it is to accept that God exists, creates and loves us. It is of greatest importance to know that God loves his world, so that we may learn also to love it. It is this world that God asks us to delight in and to find his presence in. A regaining of this vision of a world where God is present, and that in him we live and move and have our being, is an opening of our eyes to the reality that we have often lost.

> To see a world in a Grain of Sand,
> And Heaven in a Wild Flower,
> Hold Infinity in the palm of your hand,
> And Eternity in an hour.
> (William Blake, 1757–1827)

It is not only the Scriptures that are to open our eyes to God; it is the world in which we live. It opens our lives to the beyond in our midst and can free us from chasing trivial pursuits. It brings us a joy and a freedom which we cannot manufacture or buy, a freedom that St Paul calls the 'glorious freedom of the children of God'. The Celtic part of the Church used to say there are three Scriptures: the New Testament, which can only be fully understood through the Old Testament; the Old Testament which can only be fully understood through the Primary Scriptures; and the Primary Scriptures, the world itself through which God speaks to us. It is the person who is at home in the world with God that is truly at home.

## Exercises

1  Think on these words:

Gregory of Nyssa said: 'Who surveying the whole scheme of things, is so childish so as not to believe that there is a divinity in everything, clothed in it, embracing it, residing in it? For everything that is depends on Him-who-is.'

Two worlds are in the picture. Keep the whole picture in view, else the story will go wrong . . . On the earthly side just a stable, a manger, the cattle in the stalls, a woman wrapping her baby in swaddling clothes. Nothing of wonder in it. Nothing of awe. Until the world from which He came flashes in upon the scene . . .

Remember it is all one story, all one picture . . . we believe in it alright. But we are dull and slow of heart. We let it slip out of view. And so our picture gets out of focus. Unless we keep habitually in mind that other world, that eager, interested, enthusiastic world, its very wonder and beauty tend to separate it from us, to make the picture of the angels from Heaven rather misty and cloud-like beside that of the manger and the Baby on earth. Now that must not be. Any haziness as to the reality and close presence of that world puts the whole story out of gear.                    ( J. Patterson-Smyth, p. 25)

2 Read the parable of the treasure hidden in a field (Matthew 13.44).

**Pause, Presence, Picture, Ponder, Promise**

**Pause**  Allow yourself to relax. Take a time out from what you are doing and enter into a stillness and peace that is always there. Do not let the events that are just past or those to come invade this time of peace. Check your body slowly from head to foot, bit by bit, and make sure there are no tension points.

Relax as you would in the sunshine or in a warm bath. Know that only you have the power to relax your body in this way and ease the busyness of your mind. Let the stillness be part of your being.

**Presence**  Affirm the reality that you are in the presence, in the peace and in the power of God. You cannot make this happen, for it is a reality, but you can become more aware of its truth. 'The Lord is with you.' If you are willing to come to him he is there and seeking to enfold you in his love. There is no need for words, rest in God as you would with a loved one. If your mind wanders bring it back. If it wanders from the Presence too much you might like to use these words from the Hebrides and say them quietly:

> God to enfold me,
> God to surround me,
> God in my speaking,
> God in my thinking.
> God in my sleeping,
> God in my waking,

God in my watching,
God in my hoping.
God in my life,
God in my lips,
God in my soul,
God in my heart.
(*Carmichael*, 1976, p. 53)

Remember this is not a request, it is a reality. Once you have made this prayer a few times you can enter into this awareness by just using the first word of each line in a loving way, 'God'.

**Picture**   Think of a person wandering over the earth. Possibly he has covered this ground many times. It is not all that special to him: it is only a bit of ground. Then he gets a glimpse of something special; just below the surface there is something that bears looking at. He can only see a tiny piece but he wants to look closer. In this bit of ordinary land he finds a treasure, a wealth he did not dream of, lying there just below the surface. He knows he wants to make it his own. He covers the treasure back over and sells all that he has and goes and buys the field. Everyone says he has paid over the odds for it. Was it really worth the price? But he knows he is exchanging what he has for something far more precious. He buys the field though it costs him dearly and the treasure is now his. You may be able to picture this with a story of a modern treasure hunter or someone who makes a find with a metal detector.

**Ponder**   Could this man be me? Do I wander over the earth unaware of the treasure that is there just below the surface? Jesus said the kingdom of God is like this treasure. God is here in our lives. God's love seeks to enfold us. God's strength is offered to us. We can enter into his peace. But so often we tread the earth totally unaware. The kingdom of God is there all the time waiting for us to be enriched by it. Eternal life is offered to us. Because we live so often in the shallows we do not perceive the depths of our being and the world about us. Look how the man 'sacrificed' to buy the field. Is it sacrifice to give up something for something far better? Why choose to live on this one surface when our lives have such depth and meaning? Is it not worth exchanging a few temporal things and a bit of time itself to experience and share in the eternal?

**Promise** that you will spend more time each day seeking to be aware of what is about you and what the world offers to you. Seek to spend a fixed amount of time each day rejoicing in the love and presence of God.

3 Pray: 'Glory to God for all things' (John Chrysostom, *c*. 347–407)

> O thou transcendent,
> Nameless, the fibre and the breath,
> Light of the light, shedding forth universes, thou
>     centre of them,
> Thou mightier centre of the true, the good, the loving,
> Thou moral, spiritual fountain – affection's source –
>     thou reservoir,
> (O pensive soul of me – O thirst unsatisfied – waitest
>     not there?
> Waitest not haply for us somewhere there the
>     Comrade perfect?)
> Thou pulse – thou motive of the stars, suns, systems,

That, circling, move in order, safe, harmonious,
Athwart the shapeless vastnesses of space,
How should I think, how breathe a single breath, how
    speak, if, out of myself,
I could not launch, to those, superior universes?

              (Walt Whitman, quoted in *The SPCK Book of*
                         *Christian Prayer*, 1995)

# Sons and Daughters

When we call God 'Father', and more so if we say 'Abba', which is the word for Father in the Lord's Prayer and means 'Daddy', we are making a statement about relationships. We are declaring we are children of God, sons and daughters, and his home is our home: we are at home with him in this world. We are not created out of chance but out of love and for love. We are not on this earth to be slaves to a dominant master. We are not created as robots that have to do everything we are told and have no mind of their own. We have been given freedom and the ability to choose for ourselves. This freedom involves the ability to make mistakes and go the wrong way that may be bad for us, but to have no freedom at all would be much worse. In our relationship with God he does not force his will upon us but gives us the glorious freedom of the children of God. We are not asked to perform for him like a circus animal or a pet that is trained in obedience and taught a few tricks to please. We are asked to live in a loving relationship that gives us amazing freedom. St Augustine recognizes this when he says, 'Love God and do what you will.' This does not give us carte blanche to do whatever we please but we can do whatever does not go against the love that is bestowed upon us. We are asked to love God and to show that love by the way we deal with him and his creation. More than obey, we are called to delight with him in his world. We are to live righteously, that is in a right relationship with God and all that he has made. If we get our relationship with God wrong then we will have a wrong relationship to the world. If we get our relationship with each other or the world wrong, we will also have a wrong relationship with God. If we are disruptive or neglectful in the house it affects the whole household. If we cannot be trusted in our relationship then trust breaks down. Yet in all true relationships we are given the opportunity to be ourselves and to grow. A relationship that has too many rules and restrictions is in danger of dying.

The first story in the Bible of humans on the earth is about relationships. There is recognition that it is not good for humans to be alone. Living is about relationships. There is an opportunity to make a relationship with the other living things, with the world, but this is not enough for humans. Life needs to be expressed in mutual sharing and giving, not in dominance but in love. There is a suggestion that the first couple are part of each other and incomplete without each other. Yet they are able to stand alone and decide for themselves. Even in a world where male dominance was the custom you hear that the man does not always make the decisions but also follows the lead! The first people are given the freedom of choice and free will, the whole world is theirs; they can enjoy it all. There is a small restriction and it is about loving trust. The couple are left with almost complete freedom and they destroy it. They betray the trust, they go against their Creator and so not only is a relationship impaired but also the relationship with each other and all of creation is altered. They lose a sense of the Presence of the Lord not because he has gone away but because they seek to hide themselves and what they have done from him. The state of bliss, of Eden, is over.

This story is about creation, trust and love. It does not tell us how the world was made, but rather by whom it is made and who sustains it. The story is more of poetry than science. It cannot be used as a blueprint for measuring creation in a week or for the ordering of creation. It can lead us to think of the mystery of creation and the 'not by what but by whom' it is created. This moves us away from thinking of random chance or mindless mechanism to a world of meaning and purpose: it brings before us a world of love. Here we are told we come from God and we belong to God. We also learn that God is in his creation and is concerned for it. The early creation story has much to tell us about relationships and trust and it is well worth spending some time with and seeking to understand how it relates to us. You will find the story at the beginning of the Bible in Genesis 2 and 3.

In St John's first Epistle he declares 'See what love the Father has given us, that we should be called children of God; and that is what we are' (1 John 3.1). To be sons and daughters of God is to say we belong to him and are loved by him. It also implies we are to show at least some of the characteristics of our Father. Love can only grow if there is some response. We are aware of the saying, 'You cannot love a brick wall.' Let us look at five possible relationships and some misconceptions about what a good relationship is.

The first relationship can be hardly called one: it is where there is no contact at all. To know about someone is not the same as knowing them. It is no use being able to make fine theological statements about God if we do not have a living relationship with him. I know people who like to talk about God but do not talk to him. For this reason I am always worried about study groups that talk about the Scriptures but do not relate to God. It is no use having fine definitions of God if we do not draw near to him in love. The area of no contact is when everyone goes their own way and no one meets – this can hardly be called a relationship.

Once I knew two men who were brothers and farmed together. They were both very strong-minded. Soon after their father died they had a falling-out and refused to work together or speak to each other. They divided the farm and the house and continued in this pattern for years. Though they had mutual friends and saw each other they had no proper contact. They were not on speaking terms. When the time came for them to leave the farm, of which they were only tenants, they were given a house on the estate of the owner, a house to share. From the outset each had demarcation lines that the other was not allowed to cross. In their sitting room there were definite areas belonging to one or the other. Almost as a protest one became ultra-tidy and pernickety and the other became more and more dirty and slovenly. They had separate bedrooms that they almost lived in. The kitchen they shared begrudgingly but only prepared their own food and ate alone. They were two very sad men. This was no way to live for it stunted life: lack of contact is not a relationship at all.

This is true of all relationships, including marriage. We must have living contact with each other. There are times when we might avoid eye contact or refuse to speak to each other. There are even times when we might prefer to be alone, but for this to continue spells disaster. A relationship with no contact is a relationship that has already broken down, if it ever existed. To say you believe in God and yet have no contact is madness. At the lowest level you should court God, seek him and give him some attention. You will soon discover if you seek to draw near that he will draw near to you. Even when we break with God he continues to love us, waiting until we turn back to him.

The second pattern of relationship is very common and it is one of dominance. It is the pattern of a bullying father. In the case of marriage it is a domineering husband or wife. Here relationships are restricted to 'on my terms'. Unless we get our own way we refuse to cooperate. Everything has to centre round what we want. This should not be the relation of sons and daughters for it is the slave-and-master relationship. This is a servile relationship. Some people would be better suited with a robot or a puppet! There are many marriages like this where one is always dominant and the other servile. Some couples even boast that they never have a wrong word and that they always agree! Can this be real life? I can remember one lovely occasion when I was talking to a couple in their home. The husband, who was a very strong character, said, 'You know, we never have a wrong word between us.' The husband missed the wife's rather cutting reply. She said, 'If you say so, dear!'

I am a great believer in disciplining children at an early age. But I hate to hear a parent say to a child, 'I will not love you if you do that.' Nine times out of ten the child will test us and hopefully discover that despite what he or she has done the child is still loved and accepted. God may hate the sin but he still loves the sinner. A child has to learn that even though it can cause harm to relationships by refusing to cooperate for the family's well-being, the love it receives will not diminish. I love the verse from that famous passage on love – 1 Corinthians 13 – where we are told that love 'does not insist on its own way' (verse 5). We all need to take this to heart. How many marriages have broken down because a partner has demanded his or her rights – and how many couples have divorced quite legally because they did not get their rights? Usually the marriage had broken down before that. The relationship of love breaks down when a person demands rights or is ever demanding. No longer does love prevail but instead there is a desire to possess and command. So much of what the world calls love is this desire to take, possess and control for our own ends. When the word 'my' is used to express affection it is a wonderful word but it can also be used as if people were possessed like a thing. There is always a danger of talking about 'my husband', 'my wife', 'my children' as if they were possessions and not people in their own right.

Many people who talk of God seek in their own way a relationship of dominance. They do not want a loving relationship so much as one where they are in control. All prayer becomes mini-orders asking God to do this and that. There are people who want God as a puppet who will dance when they pull the strings. I once heard of a courtroom where there was a wooden crucifix and when sentence was announced the Christ figure was made to nod or shake his head in agreement. This is surely blasphemy and no way to deal with the living God. There are some who go to the extent of falling out with God because he did not do what they wanted. It is interesting how prayer can only develop when it gets beyond the asking stage. God already knows our needs. Have we also learnt to say 'your will be done' not out of servility but out of love? This is what St Paul calls the 'service which is perfect freedom'. Our God is not a control freak but one who seeks to set us free.

The opposite of dominance is 'I will only do what you want.' The roles are now reversed and the person wants to be fathered or mothered. Such people have no will of their own. They would like to escape from all responsibility and effort and become shadows or reflections of another. They hide behind another person and take on no responsibility. When a dominant person has a submissive partner it can often look ideal but in this there is little room for real mutual growth. One of the regular sayings of Christ is: 'Those who want to save their life will lose it, and those who lose their life for my sake will find it.' My first reaction to this is that you can only have a self to offer to God if you have a self. You must develop as a person in your own right. I am sure Christ does not want us to lose our identity, even though there is a call to move away from self-control and an invitation to measure life without seeking advantage to self. We are not asked to cease to be the individuals we are, created as, for every single human is unique. In the ordering of

creation God has made us like no other; we are made to be ourselves. God does not seek to absorb us into the divine as Hindus
would have us believe. To be so absorbed is to disappear. If we
cease to be individuals we cease to be fully human. Christians
have emphasized the point of our individuality when they talk
of the 'resurrection of the body' for in this is implied the continuation of the individual. If we as persons in our own right
do not rise as who we are, then we do not rise at all. Again this
must make us look at who we are. The Christian way of life
wants us to become more uniquely ourselves as we are intended
to be and this includes knowing the glorious freedom of children of God.

Our God treasures our uniqueness or he would have cloned
us rather than created every one of us in our own uniqueness.
Even identical twins though they may look the same are not
totally alike. In our relationship with him God wants us to be
ourself. The person who wants to be fathered or (s)mothered is
often weak in him- or herself. These people seek to avoid the
pressures of the world, the problems of life, and look for an
escape route from the realities around them by hiding in the
'peace of God'. There are times in life when we all need to do
this but such a refuge is meant to become also a launching pad
that sends us out again. We all need to have our energies and
strengths renewed in the love of God but that is so we can also
continue with our tasks and our daily living. God wants us to
have and to exercise our God-given freedom.

The next is often paraded as an ideal relationship. Here both
lives are one so that neither has an identity of their own. They
cannot act or survive by themselves. Because this is near the
truth, we look at a union where the two are inseparable as if it
were ideal. It is the 'I'll have to ask the wife' approach or the
'Wait until I see what the boss says'. Great but surely you are still
free to do things on your own? 'I have to ask my husband', but

surely he lets you think for yourself and go out on your own? We need to reach out in trust. When God put Adam and Eve in the Garden of Eden, he did not ask them to forever say, 'Can we do that?' He gave them freedom – a freedom that was of love and trust. If we cannot let our partner go, our love is unable to grow. Our love should set us free, not bind us. There is a danger in marriage that the marriage bond can become bondage for both rather than a binding together.

Some talk of God's will in this way. They are forever second-guessing what God wants. In itself this is not bad but it often turns out God wants what they want and I am not sure who is in bondage! Very often we do not know the will of God, though we know quite well what God does not want. I used to meet with a religious group who were forever seeking God's will for each other in their meetings. They frightened me to death, not in their seeking of God's will but in their knowing it so clearly. When I met with them they always knew what God wanted me to do! I would not have minded that if it did not always turn out to be what they wanted! Because they and God were one they knew what was good for me. Sometimes in their wisdom and caring they were right but I found them scary and in the end could not cope with them. We have not to confuse the Godhead with our own ways; we are not to blame God for all our actions.

There is still another way. It is the way for ideal relationships. It is hard to tie down for it is ever changing and moving. It is where we recognize each other for who we are, what we are and where we are. We have a large common area of action yet also a large area of individuality and freedom. Such a relationship should enrich and transform us into even more free and unique beings. This is the love that 'changes everything'. This is the love that transforms the beast and releases the prince from captivity as a frog. This is the love that wakens Sleeping Beauty and brings spring back to the garden of the Selfish Giant. Without this love the human is reduced to a thing or acts in sub-human ways. Without this love we are fettered and bound like slaves, restricted. This is the love that transforms and frees, that gives life and supplies well-being. Much of modern psychology would say that love is the power that enables you to be yourself. A baby can go through hells of deprivation if it feels unloved. To feel unloved does endless damage to our being. Teenagers who are given almost anything they want except love and attention often head for trouble. Often their rebellion is a cry for someone to notice them and is a need to be loved. It is amazing how adults' ability and output will drop if they feel that love has gone from their lives. True love is life-enhancing and energy-giving.

I remember an elderly lady in hospital for a minor operation. She appeared healthy and well but her wound would not heal. The doctor and nurses were puzzled at her body's inability to restore itself. One nurse suddenly realized the elderly lady had no visitors; she felt lonely and neglected. As I visited the hospital I was informed of this and mentioned it to those who knew her. Soon a group of her neighbours were calling on her and bringing her small gifts. They told her how they had missed her in their small community. Suddenly she felt she belonged and was loved and at the same time healing began and was rapid. Love frees us to live wholesome lives.

St Paul in 1 Corinthians 13 suggests that no matter what he does it counts for little without love. But as we are sons and daughters of God we are not without love and the love that God gives is unconditional. For us to enjoy God's love all we are asked to do is love in return. Even when we turn away from him, God's love is there waiting for us to return. Sometimes in this love we can act without any recourse to God, and at other times we will refuse to do something for it is against the love of God.

We are given freedom and it is limited only by our love. Laws are needed when our hearts are hardened and our vision of this love clouded.

The Christian Church has expressed the importance of being a person in our own right through the doctrine of the Trinity. In the Godhead itself we talk of 'three persons' yet one God. The identities of the Father, the Son and the Holy Spirit are not absorbed by each other, are not lost in confusion with the other. Each is described as a person in his own right. I believe that this is not creating God in our own image, though using our language to describe God, but recognizing that what is important in our being a person in our own right is enshrined in the very being of God. We can only offer our lives to God if we have a life to offer. God does not want things, he does not want offerings: he wants a relationship with you as you are now, not even as you hope to be but as you are now.

## Exercises

1 Thoughts

> I learned that love was our Lord's meaning.
> And I saw for certain, both here and elsewhere,
> that before ever he made us, God loved us;
> and that his love has never slackened,
> nor ever shall.
> In this love all his works have been done,
> and in this love he has made everything serve us;
> and in this love our life is everlasting.
> Our beginning was when we were made,
> but the love in which he made us never had
>     beginning.
> In it we have our beginning.

All this we shall see in God for ever.
May Jesus grant this.

> (Julian of Norwich, 1342–*c.* 1416, quoted in
> *The SPCK Book of Christian Prayer*, 1995)

Life is our most precious gift from God and we are called to make it most truly human. Neither a sub-human life, nor one that is simply passive, is a fully human life. The Hebrew conception of life is always movement and enjoyment. The evangelist John speaks of eternal life as the true life. But to John, eternal life is not the future resurrected life of believers; it is a life that we already presently enjoy in our earthly existence. Eternal life begins now when we live out Jesus' words of enduring life: 'Love one another.' Our life is one, so there is no division between physical life and spiritual life, between our life of food and drink and our life of relationship to God and neighbour.

The resurrection of Jesus announces that true life is available to, and the right of, all human beings; it is not something reserved for a few, or something that we await to happen on the 'last day': it is something we already live now. It is not compensation for the miseries of life, but a continuation of an earthly existence lived out according to God's will and purpose for humanity.

> (Fabella, 1992, pp. 189–90)

2 Read the story of the Prodigal Son in Luke 15.11–32.

### Pause, Presence, Picture, Ponder, Promise

**Pause** Stop all that you are doing and be still. Allow the stillness to enter into your heart and mind.

You might like to enter the stillness by saying:

> I weave a silence on to my lips
> I weave a silence into my mind
> I weave a silence within my heart
> I close my ears to distractions
> I close my eyes to attractions
> I close my heart to temptations.
> Calm me, O Lord, as you stilled the storm
> Still me, O Lord, keep me from harm
> Let all the tumult within me cease
> Enfold me, Lord, in your peace.
>
> (Adam, 1985, p. 7)

Rest in the presence and peace of God, know he offers himself to you as he offers these gifts. There is no need for effort. Make sure your body is relaxed and your mind rested. Breathe in slowly and deeply. If the mind wants to wander, with each breath in affirm: 'The Lord is here.' As you exhale, affirm: 'His Spirit is with us.'

**Presence**   Allow the love of God to enfold you. Immerse yourself in the love of God. Know that even when you lose your grip on God he has you in his hands. As being aware of God and his love is of the utmost importance, spend a good part of this time rejoicing in his presence.

**Picture**   Visualize the story as if it was a film. See the young son making his demands and causing much unhappiness. The sale of one's inheritance is painful unless we are insensitive. Watch how the son turns away with his back to his father and sets off. The father stands watching with sadness but knows his son must venture. The father could have made him stay but he wanted him to have freedom of choice. If he were to stay it would have to be out of love.

Now see the son in a far country. Money buys him a lot of fun. He is having a great adventure. But his resources, though many, are limited. His supplies run out and famine comes. Now he is not much better than an animal; he feeds with pigs. What is worse he is on his own and without love. His memories of good times are at work. He realizes he is living below par. He would be far better where he was loved. He decides to turn – at this point is it a resurrection that begins? He is aware of his unworthiness but he is also aware of his father's love.

Look at the return. See how the father has been waiting and runs to meet the Prodigal's return. He hugs him, kisses him, clothes him, provides a feast for him. He is accepted as a son returned. It is like being given new life, a return from the dead.

Now look at the other son with a face like thunder. He refuses to come in. He talks of slavish obedience – is there a hint of jealousy here? How unaware of his father's love he seems. Is he not aware of the father's generosity and all that is offered to him? His anger and his whole attitude make him stay outside.

**Ponder**    Where do you fit into this story? Have you a sense of adventure? Are you willing to risk making mistakes? Dare you not leave home?

Do you know the love of the Father or are you under the Law?

How many opportunities of resurrection, of turning and of newness of life are offered to you?

Most of us have been both the Prodigal and the one who lived under law and failed to recognize love. We need to discover the world of grace where God's love and God himself are not earned but freely given. Our actions can hurt love but the love of God is not destroyed. God welcomes you today.

**Promise**  to seek and enjoy the presence of God each day – to be at home with God in your home and to live in the kingdom of God which is at hand.

3  Pray

> O Love, O God, who created me, in your love recreate me.
> O Love who redeemed me, fill up and redeem for yourself in me
> whatever part of your love has fallen into neglect within me.
> O Love, O God, who, to make me yours, in the blood of your Christ
> purchased me, in your truth sanctify me.
> O Love, who adopted me as a daughter, after your own heart fashion and foster me.
> O Love, who as yours and not another's chose me, grant that I may
> cleave to you with my whole being.
> O Love, O God, who first loved me, grant that with my whole heart,
> and with my whole soul, and with my whole strength, I may love you.
> O Love, O God almighty, in your love confirm me.
> O Love most wise, give me wisdom in love of you.
> O Love most sweet, give me sweetness in taste of you.

*Sons and Daughters*

O Love most dear, grant that I may live for you alone.
O Love most faithful, in all my tribulations comfort
and succour me.
O Love who is ever with me, work all my works in me.
O Love most victorious, grant that I may persevere to
the end in you.

(Gertrude of Thuringen, 1256–*c.* 1303)

# *Not at Home*

We have been talking of realities when we speak of a wonderful world that is Presence-filled, of a world created out of love and for love. The kingdom of God is here for us to enjoy, God himself is here for us to enjoy. As the Westminster Catechism says: 'The chief end of man is to enjoy God and glorify him forever.' When we are at home in both kingdoms we are able to delight in the world and be at home with God. We acknowledge that we are created beings but that we are able to act as co-creators with God. The living in two kingdoms is a life-extending venture and a joy of knowing that the two are one in God.

But in this world that is only part of the reality, for often we are not at home with God. We choose to exercise our God-given freedom and to turn away from him. Perhaps the only way to express our freedom is to show we can go whichever way we choose! From the very start of the Scriptures in Genesis we hear that the humans choose not to obey God. To turn away from God is to turn away from the source of our life, to turn away from light and love, and yet we all choose to do this at some time. In Genesis this is expressed as the humans leaving their first home, Eden.

Gerard Manley Hopkins expresses something of this choice in his poem 'God's Grandeur':

> The world is charged with the grandeur of God,
> It will flame out, like shining from shook foil;

It gathers to a greatness, like ooze of oil
Crushed. Why do men then now not reck his rod?
Generations have trod, have trod, have trod;
And all is seared with trade: bleared, smeared with toil;
And wears man's smudge and shares man's smell: the soil
Is bare now, nor can foot feel, being shod.
And for all this, nature is never spent;
There lives the dearest freshness deep down things.

(Gerard Manley Hopkins, 1844–89)

We are given the chance to be at home with God but we are not always at home with him and we live in a world that is not at home with him. The Bible always faces the realities of life. It is not a story of happy families or enduring relationships but rather of struggle, and often of people and nations making wrong choices. In expressing their freedom the first humans lose their close relationship with God. The first family sees one son murder another. Relationships are forever moving and changing and are often far from the ideal; this is the real world.

The first time I left home, I wanted to assert my freedom, my independence. I was asserting my free will. There was something I did not want to do. I am sure it was something quite trivial that I was expressing, I cannot even now remember what it was. Whatever, it made me determined to leave home. I was eight or nine at the time. My father helped me to pack a case. There were no harsh words, only what seemed a willingness to let me go. I now suspect he filled the case with anything heavy that he could find. He took me to the gate and watched me struggle down the street. By the time I got to the bottom of the street the case was a burden and I was exhausted. I sat on the case and tears began to fall. I was hoping no one would notice. But my father had been watching and after a while he came to where I was and said, 'Hello, you haven't got very far. Do you want to come home?' Of course I did. He picked up the case and we returned to a welcome by my mother. I experienced the ability to walk out if I wanted to but also the loss in going. I also was made aware of the love that welcomed me back. Through a loving home I was learning of the love of God, though his name was rarely mentioned.

The necessity of growing up, becoming independent, of deciding who we are and to whom – if anyone – we belong is incumbent upon all of us. It is right that the day must come for most of us to leave home. Ideally it is a place we will remember always as a place of love, and we will desire to return to it every so often. If we are fortunate we will leave it in good grace and not with hostility. I had to leave to grow: to know I was free. Love is shown in letting go. I thought of the time I left home when I read the poem 'Walking Away' by C. Day Lewis:

How selfhood begins with a walking away,
And love is proved in the letting go.
(C. Day Lewis, 1904–72)

In the story of the Prodigal Son you see someone not at home with his family. As he is the younger son there is little doubt about what will be rightly his: according to the Scriptures he is to have one third of the property when his father dies, the older son will have two thirds (Deuteronomy 21.17). Only sometimes will this be given to a son while the father lives, and then it will be given on the condition that he looks after his father. Many a father rues the day he gives all to his children; note the words of King Lear as he feels uncared for by his children:

How sharper than the serpent's tooth it is
To have a thankless child!
(*King Lear*, Act 1 scene 5)

37

In the story of the Prodigal we have a young man who does not appreciate what he has. He thinks lightly of his inheritance and wants to move away to the attraction of the city. I have known many a farmer's son who has done this only to return home and be glad to be back. There is a movement in many lives from being sick of home to becoming homesick. What we inherit is a gift from the generations before us. Often at an early stage we do not fully appreciate it because we have not worked for it. In the year 1274 Peter the Monk was complaining:

> The young people of today think of nothing but themselves. They have no reverence for parents or old age. They are impatient of all restraint. They talk as if they knew everything, and what passes as wisdom with us is foolishness with them. As for the girls they are foolish and immoderate in speech, behaviour and dress.

Such a description would seem to fit the Prodigal Son very well as it seems to fit almost any age and time. The young son would inherit his portion of the estate not only for his own use but also for the use of future generations; the land is meant to be handed on in the family. He was expected to hand it on to his son as his father had given it to him. The earth is not just ours. It belongs to the past and the future. The way we are using many of the earth's resources and changing its eco-balance must be weighed against what we are leaving for others to inherit. As the world is not ours alone, we cannot do what we like with it. Our freedom brings with it some responsibilities. Too often we are ready to sell our future for an immediate gain. The Scriptures are well aware of this. One of the early stories is about Esau and Jacob. Esau gave his birthright away to his brother for a bowl of lentil stew (Genesis 25.29–34). We may smile at this but many times in our life we sacrifice our heritage for minor gains and we trade the eternal for that which is passing away. In asking for his rights and selling them the Prodigal Son would bring shame and disgrace upon his family.

In a sense what is worse is asking for his inheritance; it is as good as wishing the father dead. 'I want what you can give me now. It is no use waiting until you die, I want to enjoy myself now. I do not need you in my life. I am grown up and I want my freedom.' How much antagonism is here? How many children in anger have said to a parent, 'I wish you were dead'? There is sadness in the breakdown of relationships. Those who have become so self-centred that they are unaware of what their actions are doing to others cause much pain. At its extreme the self-centred do not even care as long as they get their own way. This is truly what sin is and it is portrayed by the defying of God in Eden, and again in the killing of Abel by Cain. This is where the crucifixion begins. The 'wish you were dead' syndrome has its fullest expression in the crucifixion, where humans are allowed to edge God himself out of the city and out of their lives, to fix and kill the God of love. We can choose to turn our backs on love and sensitivity and so wreak havoc in the world. Any who are insensitive to the love of God or of humans become a danger to themselves and the world. The story of the Holocaust and the extermination of millions of Jews is an illustration of not only individuals but also of nations becoming too insensitive and determined to have their own way. Whenever we treat others or God as a means to our own ends this danger appears.

The young man wants to leave home as he says, 'Give me'. This is a scene that could come from any time in history. The son is seeking his freedom. He wants to branch out on his own, yet not without the resources he can get. He does not want to go empty-handed even if it means the diminishment of his family. He demands his rights, though at this stage he has none except by the grace and goodness of his father. He wants his freedom but in truth can only have it through the goodwill of his father. This is a son not a slave. The father does not seek to tie him down but no doubt regrets his departure. Love is shown in letting go. The going away must have grieved the father and it would have humbled him in the eyes of his neighbours.

In many parts of the world, including where Jesus was speaking, they would have found this story incredible. Fathers are not like that. They are rulers in their own right, and sons are meant to obey. There are many people who still view God in this light and see him as a despotic father rather than a loving God who gives freedom. Most of those who heard Jesus would have suggested the father should have given his son a good beating to teach him a lesson. He could have disinherited him and just let him go but not allowed him to take anything with him. The chapter in Deuteronomy that tells of how to divide an inheritance between sons ends in a severe way. It suggests that a rebellious son should be brought before the elders for his riotous living and stoned to death (Deuteronomy 21.18–21)! Inheritance is not to be squandered or wasted, do so at your peril. Yet Jesus has introduced into this situation a father who is deeply loving and willing to give his children their freedom. This is very dangerous – freedom always is – but the alternatives are worse.

There are many reasons for leaving home and often it is right and necessary. To leave the support and protection of home and stand on our own feet is a necessary part of growing up and extending ourselves. We leave home to take on a new job or to get married and make a home of our own. We leave because we have a feeling that there must be more to life than this. Sometimes the leaving is caused by an inner restlessness, a searching for the ideal. Using the words from Shakespeare's

*Antony and Cleopatra* in a different way, 'We have immortal longings.' At other times we leave as rebels with the less noble thought, 'If this is my home then I am sick of it.'

I can remember when I left home to train for the priesthood. How people praised the sacrifice I was making! I was giving up a job with pay, I was giving up nights out with the lads, I was going away from the pop culture into a monastic setting: how noble, how sacrificial. It would have been easy to gloat in their admiration. But I was giving up something for what I saw as something better. I was doing what I felt I wanted to do: what I was called to do. For me it was fulfilling and not negating. The sacrifice was not on my part but on that of my parents. They could have done with my help at home. They could have benefited from the extra income I was bringing in. There was no apparent gain for them and there was certainly a loss. Yet in love they encouraged me, they let me go. Even more, they tried to give me a little financial support out of their small income. I learnt of grace and love through their actions. I left home with the blessing and love of my parents.

Often our not being at home is due to being self-centred: this can stop us being at home even when we are at home. The Prodigal says, 'Give me'. He wants to take without the responsibilities that go along with the gift. He wants to go his own way regardless of others and without respect to his father. He knows what he wants and he demands that he gets it. How often in life have we found ourselves in similar situations? It is when we seek to be in control regardless; this is the way to dominate and to conquer. It is not the way of love. Such an attitude separates us from the world of grace and love and enters a world of law and commands, not imposed upon us but created by ourselves. When self-will rules we choose to step out of the kingdom of God and go our own way. We often then break with the Father. We live in a world that has no reference to God or his grace. Many can say with St Augustine:

> How different are my days
> from the days of the Lord!
> They are 'my' days
> because I took them for myself,
> intoxicated as I was by my reckless independence
> which led me to abandon him.
>
> (Watts, 1987, p. 26)

Though it is very necessary to have a self, when the self becomes all-important we are in danger of seeking to live in a world of our own creation. In this state we are in danger of walking away from or stepping outside the kingdom of God that is offered to us.

For a while it was fashionable to say, 'We have come of age; God is dead.' There is no need to make reference to the out-moded idea of God. God has always given us this freedom. He does not force his love or his will upon us. He wants us to choose. Often it seems the only choice that people make is to walk away. The guidance of the past is tossed aside: Scriptures and ancient wisdom go unheeded. We are creating our own world. But for most this is like going on a journey and throwing away the maps and the compass and just guessing where to go next. Without accepting guidance people soon become lost and distressed, and their view on life becomes distorted. In the world of self there is no one to turn to and there is little grace. The world of the self-centred is always in danger of living by the law of the jungle where might is right and where all strive to dominate. Using the word carefully, in the end the self-centred world, the world without God, is hell. I well remember my mother saying at some point after I had been causing some distress at home: 'You know God created heaven and earth, only we can create hell.' To turn away from God is to turn towards the darkness – yet in our testing of freedom we will do it. I have had to learn and relearn that this earth and heaven are gifts to us from God. I cannot create them. I can only accept them in grace. At the same time I know that I am capable of creating hell whenever I turn my back on God and his grace.

Life is meant to be an adventure. When we cease to reach out and stretch ourselves something in us dies or we become frustrated; for life to be lived to the full it has to be adventurous. I believe that God calls us to adventure, to extend ourselves and to seek new horizons. God wants us to be someone for he has made each of us as a unique being. We all have something, different talents, to offer to God that no one else can. Above all he wants us to give ourselves to him as he gives himself to us. He wants us to share our life with him and with each other. Our God is the God who makes all things new and he wants us to walk in newness of life. A relationship with God will extend our vision, our sensitivity and indeed our whole life. Whenever life gets static or dull God calls us out to risk and to be renewed. We must realize that not every moving out is wrong. It is just as dangerous never to leave home. When we look at the end of the story of the Prodigal Son the most frightening person is the son who does not leave home.

Every now and again something happens in our lives to challenge us, or to make us change direction. For many people the highlight of this experience is when they meet their loved one for the first time and feel a great attraction. True love is not just a desire to satisfy ourselves. There is much of this love around and it parades itself as true love. True love is when we are so enraptured by the other that we want to give our life to that person. We want to share our lives, not to absorb or possess each other but to become one in a way that enhances each of our freedoms and our lives. It is for this reason that most people learn of the great Other who is God and his love through the love of their loved ones. It is when we treat another with the respect and care that is called for that the Other who is God is also there to be discovered. At least once in our lives there is a person or an event for which we would give up everything; such giving up is not sacrifice for it is the leaving of one thing for something better. To make such a move is not to deny ourselves but rather to find fulfilment in our newly found life; it is to reach out and extend ourselves. This is a call to awaken out of sleep, to arise out of a self-centred life and live fully in the present; it is to know that you have arrived and are where you should be. When we awaken in this way, we become at home in the world and the world itself becomes Presence-filled. It is a call to live beyond the limits of our own centre and to reach out to the other. When asked, 'What makes a man or woman leave his or her parents?' the Bible answers, 'Love'. But we must remember this is the ideal; too many separate themselves from home or others for their own selfish ends.

The young son in his leaving home is not truly aware of what is already being offered to him. He fails to appreciate the world around him and the love that is offered. In turning his back on this, and seeking to take out but not give in return, we see the separation that is caused when we become self-centred. This is the very essence of sin, when we seek to become self-made men and women, when we refuse to see the grace and goodness of the giver and believe we are possessors in our own right. The turning our backs on love, the betrayal of love, the seeking the death of love is sin and thus we enter into the darkness of a world on our own. It often will take us a long time to discover that 'without love we are nothing'.

## Exercises

1 Thoughts

> The notion that what we happen to apprehend directly
> with our five senses is all the reality there is now seems
> to me almost grotesquely parochial. And this convic-
> tion is the bedrock of whatever religious faith I have:
> there must be more than this.
>
> (Philip Toynbee, diary entry for 26 October 1979)

> God from whom to stray is to fall,
> and to whom to return is to rise up,
> in whom to remain is to rest on a firm foundation.
> To leave you is to die,
> To return to you is to come back to life,
> To dwell in you is to live.
> No one loses you if he does not fall into error,
> no one seeks you without being called,
> no one finds you without being purified.
> To go away from you is to be lost,
> to seek you is to love,
> to see you is to make you our own.
>
> (Watts, 1987, pp. 87–8)

2 Read the parable of the invitation to the wedding feast in
Luke 14.16–24.

**Pause, Presence, Picture, Ponder, Promise**

**Pause**   Come and rest in the peace that is there behind all
the bustle of the day. Allow yourself time out from your
busyness and routine. Work is nearly always improved by
such times of relaxation. Look over your body starting from

your head, neck and shoulders; see that every part of you is relaxed and not over-tense. Immerse yourself in the quiet. Breathe in slowly and deeply; seek to be at peace with yourself.

**Presence**   Know that God is with you and invites you to enjoy his Presence, to rest in his peace and be enfolded in his love. You are invited to enter his kingdom at any time. There is a sense that God waits upon you for he will not force his way into your life. You may like to say quietly:

> You Lord are in this place,
> Your presence fills it,
> Your presence is peace.
>
> You Lord are in my life,
> Your presence fills it,
> Your presence is peace.
>
> You Lord are in my heart,
> Your presence fills it,
> Your presence is peace.

Know this is not a request but the reality that you often ignore.

**Picture**   See the king sending out invitations to a banquet. He does not want anyone to miss it so he sends out his invitations to make you aware of the coming feast. What an honour to be with the king. How wonderful to be offered marvellous food in a land where food is often scarce. What a joy it will be to celebrate with the king. No doubt you will put your invitation where it can be seen. It will serve to show others how fortunate you are and as a reminder that you are invited. Can you believe it! Some have allowed themselves to become double-booked and send in their apologies. They are excusing themselves and so excluding themselves. Listen to their excuses. They would be laughable if they were not so sad. 'I have bought a piece of land and must go and see it.' Would any sensible person buy a piece of land without looking at it? Even if he did it is bought, it is his, he could look at it tomorrow. He has excused himself. Another says, 'I have bought five yoke of oxen, and I am going to try them out.' Another lame excuse. Would you buy a car from someone without testing it? Anyhow if you have bought it the deed is done. Yet another sends in his apologies saying, 'I have just been married, therefore I cannot come.' Well, he knew the invitation was there long before; it's no use blaming his wife. I have a suspicion that this excuse may have raised a few laughs in a world where the man was seen as dominant. Places were reserved for each of these but they felt they had something better to do and so they excused themselves. The king in his generosity reaches out to others, perhaps those whom the listeners to the story found undeserving, and they came and enjoyed the feast.

**Ponder**    The excuses all have a sense of the ridiculous. The king has offered them the ability to celebrate in his kingdom and they ignore it. Look at your own excuses for putting off coming to God. Are you too busy to pray? Is Sunday a day when you feel you need to go for a drive or wash the car and cannot make it to church? Perhaps you are just too tired to pray – after a round of golf or night out at the theatre! You are invited to enjoy the presence of the king, to be part of the kingdom of God. God wants you to come. Do you make excuses and so exclude yourself? Do you turn away from God in your desire to have a 'good time'? Perhaps you have never taken up the invitation to come and celebrate in his presence. Remember there is no forcing from God, only an invitation, but those who excuse themselves exclude themselves.

**Promise**   to pick up the invitation each day and to enjoy being in the presence and in the kingdom of God. Remember if you do not make a fixed time and place for this meeting it is far less likely to take place.

3  Pray

> I find Thee throned in my heart, my Lord Jesus.
> It is enough.
> I know that thou art throned in Heaven.
> My heart and Heaven are one.
>
> (Maclean, 1937, p. 106)

> I am serene because I know Thou lovest me.
> Because Thou lovest me, naught can move me from
>    thy peace.
> Because thou lovest me, I am the one to whom all
>    good has come.
>
> (Maclean, 1937, p. 73)

# In a Far Country

In a very few words Jesus depicts the departure of the younger son and what he gets up to:

> A few days later the younger son gathered all that he had and travelled to a distant country, and there he squandered his property in dissolute living. When he spent everything, a severe famine took place throughout that country, and he began to be in need.
>
> (Luke 15.13–14)

Here is a young man who knew love and grace at home but is now in a far country. Here, he has to buy the things he wants. In this world you only get what you pay for unless you discover people who have grace and generosity. As long as he has money he has friends but when the money runs out he is on his own with no one to help him. He who has known love also knows loneliness: he experiences a great hunger and it is not just for food. If we do not experience the sublime things of our existence we will not truly experience the depths. Somehow things have gone wrong for this young man, as they do for many of us. His 'good times' do not last. At this stage many of those who heard Jesus telling the story would say, 'It serves him right! He wouldn't listen and now he must pay the consequences.' In his own way this young man was experiencing the Fall. To live in a world without love, without God, is hell. He had moved away from the grace and protection that had enabled him to live a full life. Now he suffered restrictions.

I can remember leaving my loved ones to go to a conference in the city. I was only there a week and there were crowds of people but somehow I felt utterly alone. It was not that I was among bad people but I had this feeling we were all just going through the motions to gain a few 'Brownie points' and no one had their heart in it. Somehow I felt we were not being stretched or encouraged to rise to our potential. It was as if that was too much bother.

Sin is not necessarily being terribly wicked. There are many people who justify themselves by saying they keep the commandments, they do not smoke or drink or chase after other people's partners. But I always want to know what it *is* they do. What are they on this earth for: what is the unique contribution they can make to the world? Sin can often be seen in the way we live below par. Sin means missing the bull's-eye of a target. You could well use the word 'sin' for getting a double score when you aimed at double top on the dart board and leaving it at that. Sin is when we fail to be the person we were made to be. Sin can be offering things to God – hymns and prayers – when he wants us to offer ourselves. To give less than ourselves to any situation can be a sin. Though drinking in itself may not be, and is not wrong, being under par the next day makes it wrong.

What God loves is nothing but the whole – the whole self in the whole situation. That and nothing else is what is present to God: all present. Making a present to God of one's whole self, that is love for God. Being all present, all now, that is love for God. This entails calling one's self from the past, the regrets and resentment and the scars, and presenting them to the eyes of his love. It entails calling in one's self from the future, the daydreams, the fears, ambitions, and presenting them, leaving them with him. It entails calling in the self from beyond the pale, the self that would be properly banned from one's autobiography but is a true part of the one God loves.

(Taylor, 1992, p. 278)

There are events in all our lives we would like to forget or at least leave out of our autobiography. For the Prodigal his time of starvation and his eating with the pigs must have been one of those times. Here is a free son who has become a slave. Here is a man who had dignity now eating with the swine. 'Cursed is he who feeds swine.' He has gone lower than this for he is eating the pig food. Isaiah has a picture of a nation that turned its back on God. God says 'Here am I, here am I' and holds his hands out to a rebellious people, who follow their own devices, who provoke him and eat swine's flesh (Isaiah 65.1–4). The story of the Prodigal is not a new one and it is repeated often in each generation. We are offered freedom and the kingdom of God; we choose to go the way that leads to captivity and deprivation. We are often led astray by the false promises of others who have already strayed.

The Prodigal is a man in exile from all that was truly his: he is a man in captivity. In his own being the Prodigal reflects what has happened to Israel more than once. The people of Israel were in slavery in Egypt but God brought them into freedom and into the Promised Land. Even there they rebelled against their God and once again they went into exile, this time to Babylon. The prophet Ezekiel spoke to a captive people who had lost all hope and who said: 'Our bones are dried up, and our hope is lost; we are cut off completely' (Ezekiel 37.11). But to this people in the depth of despair Ezekiel proclaimed the hope of revival and renewal through the God who cared for them. Ezekiel preached a resurrection of those who were wrung out and dried up in that wonderful passage of new life into dry bones (Ezekiel 37.1–14). The passage ends with the people being able to return to their own soil through the action of God, a reminder of how precious the land is to the Jewish people. God freed his people from captivity but most of those who listened to Jesus believed they were once again in captivity, for they were not free but living under the regime of the Roman Empire. Pagans, who restricted their freedom, imposed their way of life upon them and ruled them. Hearing Jesus speak of a son who would arise and go to his father, and of a father who would say that the Prodigal 'was dead and has come to life; he was lost and has been found' (Luke 15.32) was most likely to be seen as a reference to the freeing of Israel from captivity.

This pattern of a good life through God's grace, a misuse of what we are given and a turning away from God and going into captivity or being defeated, is a common theme throughout the book of Judges and most of the Old Testament. This is not surprising for it is a common experience of all of us. In using our freedom to turn away we turn our back on the good that is offered to us; we step outside the kingdom. Richard Holloway expresses this situation well:

All this beauty that haunts us comes by revelation to those who are able to hear it. It is all around us, pressing upon us, if only we could hear, if only we could learn to listen. And the news of that other country we are born trying to remember comes the same way. We are homesick for something that is beyond the universe yet strangely affects the movement of the sea. Our sense of regret points to a primordial homesickness – a sorrow that afflicts us precisely because we turn ourselves away from God who is the country we long for, the land of lost content. Most of us are mildly aware of this, but we are more than half afraid of the consequences of really finding God – 'Lest, having found him, we must have naught beside' in the words of Francis Thompson. The saints have a raging sense of their need for God. He is the country of their soul, and the tidings from that far country break in upon them. That is the meaning of Christ, who brought tidings, news of that country. He brought the very air of it into our land of exile. And there have been other moments of revelation, brief glimpses beyond the curtain. The world rolls back and we are left forlorn, but sustained by the memory of it and the sense that we have, included in our sense of return. (Holloway, 1984, p. 5)

Throughout the history of the searching of the human spirit this story appears again and again in many guises. The life of John Newton, the writer of the hymn 'Amazing Grace', illustrates this well. The son of a sea captain and due to have a good career at sea, he failed time and again to do his duty. He led a dissolute and depraved life. At one time he became the slave of a slave trader. He had sunk into the depths. Due to what he believed to be a miraculous escape from a storm-stricken ship, John Newton's life took a new direction. He may have done much that was wrong but now he gave himself whole-heartedly to the service of God. He would spend some of his time working for the abolition of slavery. He became ordained in the Church of England and became a hymn writer. He wrote the hymns 'How sweet the name of Jesus sounds' and 'Glorious things of thee are spoken'. But he will be best remembered for his hymn 'Amazing Grace'. Two of these verses reflect well how he felt about God's grace and goodness:

> Amazing grace! How sweet the sound
> that saved a wretch like me.

I once was lost, but now am found;
was blind but now I see.

Through many dangers, toils and snares
I have already come.
'Tis grace has brought me safe thus far,
and grace will lead me home.

John Newton died in December 1807 as the Vicar of St Mary's, Woolnoth. His last words were: 'My memory is nearly gone but I remember two things, that I am a great sinner and that Christ is a great Saviour.'

Though he had descended to the depths the Prodigal Son 'came to himself'; he realized what he was missing. As long as he stayed in this state he would become more and more distressed, disfigured and disgusted with himself. Though we can severely deface the image of God that is within us we cannot efface it totally. Though we may find ourselves distressed and feeling disfigured, we know we have someone who will accept us and love us and who can bring us peace and well-being.

There is no reason to stay where he is for the Prodigal had been born a free man. He has a loving father. When he realizes this he says, 'I will arise'. How often are we given the chance of rising from what is dull and dead, from hunger and captivity? I believe that we all have many resurrections. Resurrection, newness of life is possible through the love of the Father. 'He came to himself' describes a movement away from despair to hope. It shows a person who has had the image of God defaced but not effaced. Christians believe that everyone has a dignity that cannot be fully destroyed. No matter how much we mar the image, we are made in the image of God. No matter how far away we wander, God in his grace is there, wanting us to return to him. He wants us to enjoy the love and the freedom of his kingdom.

He may have given us much already but he wants to give us more. Only a right relationship with God will give us a right relationship with everything else. Another person who had plumbed the depths expresses this in his poem, 'The Hound of Heaven':

> I fled Him, down the nights and down the days;
> I fled Him, down the arches of the years;
> I fled Him, down the labyrinthine ways
> Of my own mind; and in the mist of tears
> I hid from Him, and under running laughter.
> Up vistaed hopes I sped;
> And shot, precipitated,
> Adown Titanic glooms of chasmed fears,
> From those strong Feet that followed, followed after.
> But with unhurrying chase,
> And unperturbed pace,
> Deliberate speed, majestic instancy,
> They beat – and a Voice beat
> More instant than the Feet –
> 'All things betray thee, who betrayest me.'
>
> (Francis Thompson, 1859–1907)

When we turn our back on God we fall, we choose to walk towards the darkness, we fail to live a full life. This is not a punishment by God, it is the natural result of the road we have chosen; but God is still there and waiting for us to come to ourselves. He has given us the power to turn and to arise. One of the great commentators on this is St Augustine:

> I was so slow to love you, Lord,
> your age-old beauty is still as new to me:
> I was so slow to love you!

You were within me,
Yet I stayed outside
seeking you there;
in my ugliness I grabbed at
the beautiful things of your creation.
Already you were with me,
but I was still far from you.
The things of this world kept me away: I did not know
    then
that if they had not existed through you
they would not have existed at all.
Then you called me
and your cry overcame my deafness;
you shone out
and your light overcame my blindness;
you surrounded me with your fragrance
and I breathed it in,
so that now I yearn for more of you;
I tasted you,
and now I am hungry and thirsty for you;
you touched me,
and now I burn with longing for your peace.

(Watts, 1987, p. 19)

In the desert of this world our lives are touched with a hunger and thirst for God. We may be in a far country but the love of God and his kingdom are never far away. The Prodigal fulfils the message that Jesus preached in Mark 1.15: 'The time is fulfilled, and the kingdom of God has come near; repent, and believe in the good news' in that he decides to turn to the Father. It takes courage to turn because it means we have to admit we having been going in the wrong direction. It takes a change of heart more than a change of place. But God has made us able to do this and he will accept us as we are. If we are living below par and outside of the kingdom the time has come to repent and this simply means to turn around, face the other way, start our journey back. God does not seek to humble us by asking us to recount all our sins, but it will require humility on our part to admit we are facing the wrong way and that many of our problems are of our own making. Remember the kingdom of God is at hand and ready to be entered. It is not to be put off until another world or even another time. It is here and now and waiting for us. To know that you are still breathing is no guarantee by itself that you are truly alive but it does mean you can still make an act of will and turn back to the Lord of life. Why stay outside the kingdom when it is there and being offered to you?

## Exercises

1 Thoughts

In preaching on Christ saying he came not for the righteous but for sinners John Donne says:

Are ye to learn now what that is? He that cannot define Repentance, he that cannot spell it, may have it; and he that has written whole books, great Volumes of it, may be without it. In one word, (one word will not do it, but in two words) it is *Aversio*, and *Conversio*; it is a turning from our sins, and a returning to God.

(Oakley, 2004, p. 8)

The words in the baptism service, 'Do you repent of your sins?' are not enough in themselves. It is necessary to see how we fail and fall short but this can leave us with a sense of darkness and failure. Some are forever repenting of their sins

and seem to delight in it! We have to follow repentance with
a turning to Christ. It is in Christ that there is newness of life:
in Christ is our resurrection. It is no use just turning away
from darkness; we turn to the love and light of Christ. Think
on these words of Augustine:

> When we confess our wretchedness to you
> and acknowledge your mercy to us,
> we are revealing your love for us,
> so that as you have begun,
> so you may complete the task of setting us free:
> that we may cease to be unhappy
> in ourselves
> and become happy in you.
>
> (Watts, 1987, p. 50)

2  Read the story of the Wise and Foolish Maidens in Matthew
   25.1–13.

**Pause, Presence, Picture, Ponder, Promise**

**Pause**  Stop all your activity, still your mind and let your
body relax. Take time to see that you are relaxed, each part of
your body, and that you are comfortable. Put all troubled
thoughts and anxiety out of your mind. If the mind wants to
wander, bring it back into the stillness with the words, 'Peace,
be still.' Enjoy the fact that you can relax.

**Presence**  Know that you are in the presence and love of
God. He enfolds you in his love. He surrounds you with his
protection and offers you life in all its fullness. Rejoice that
you are in the heart of God. He cares for you and offers you
his rest and his peace. Keep your attention on him. When the

mind wanders away, say quietly, 'The Lord is here: his Spirit is with me.' Know that this is a fact and not a request. Seek to be alert to God and to his abiding presence. Repeat often during the day the words: 'The Lord is here: his Spirit is with me'. Let them help to make you more aware of the truth that God is always with you and never leaves you.

**Picture**   See ten maidens waiting for the bridegroom to come. They are all invited, they are all given the opportunity to share in the joy of the wedding. They are all excited about it. They all have lamps to see them through the darkness. There is no suggestion that the foolish ones were wicked or evil; only that they had neglected certain things that were required of them. It was a small matter to make sure they had oil and light; they could have done it but they never bothered. The groom seems to be delayed. During the delay half of the women discover they are running out of oil. They try to borrow but that is not possible, so they leave their post and go off to get some oil. While they are away the groom comes and those who are in attendance enter with the groom into the celebrations. The doors are locked. When the others turn up and knock they are too late, they are refused entry. The groom speaks the terrible words, 'I never knew you.'

**Ponder**   How often have we made excuses for not saying our prayers and welcoming God into our homes? Often our sins are not those of great wickedness but rather of omission: 'we have left undone those things which we ought to have done'. Some things you cannot get at the last minute; this is true of learning, of character and of faith. Faith is not a set of beliefs but rather a living relationship with the One who comes. If we are not present in mind or attention, or have our interests elsewhere, then we do not build up this relationship. There comes a time when it is too late. The artist Pablo Picasso said: 'Never put off today anything you do not want to leave undone for ever.'

To live our lives without due care and proper attention courts disaster. We ignore the things of God at our peril.

Matthew puts this parable of Jesus after the entry into Jerusalem and at a time when the 'established Church' is about to reject him. The story clearly applies to the Jewish nation but it also has a universal application. We all need a living relationship with our God. Talking about him is not enough. We have to talk to him and know him as our companion and friend.

The words of the bridegroom to those clamouring to come in are a terrible statement. 'I never knew you.' Often we ask: 'Do you two know each other?' Have we taken the time and made the effort to know Jesus, to be friends with him, or have we been too preoccupied? Can Jesus say to us: 'I never knew you'?

> I come to you in love, I long for you and you turn away.
> I knock at your door and your heart and you find no room for me.
> I reach out to touch you but you remain unaware.
> I speak to you and in your life but you do not listen.

God does not exclude us from his kingdom. He has given us an open invitation. Only we can exclude ourselves by excusing ourselves or by not bothering at all. It is not, 'Do you know about God?' but rather, 'Do you know him and does he know you?'

**Promise**  that you will make space each day for God and spend time getting to know him and talking to him.

3  Pray

> God, I turn to you and your light.
> In turning to you, I turn away from darkness.
> God, I turn to you and your grace.
> In turning to you my emptiness is filled.
> God, I turn to you and your power.
> In turning to you my weakness is made strong.
> God, I turn to you and your forgiveness.
> In turning I am renewed, refreshed, restored.
> God, I turn to you and your love.
> In turning to you I enter into your love and life
>     eternal.

# Lovers Meeting

Throughout our lives many of us realize that when we have nowhere else to turn we can at least go home. If we are fortunate we know that we are loved by at least our dear ones. There we are aware of their goodness, forgiveness and acceptance. It is a love that is not earned or deserved but of the kingdom of grace, a love offered without reserve. You cannot buy this love but it is freely offered to you. Though you may have pained this love, rejected this love, turned your back on this love, there you are still welcomed home. Such love is not without cost for it involves sacrifice and the giving of self. At its fullest it is seen in the crucifixion, where God gives himself for love of the world. St John the Divine in the book of Revelation has a very telling few words when he describes Jesus as 'the Lamb that was slaughtered from the foundation of the world' (Revelation 13.8, marginal note). Whenever anyone has turned away from the love of God, there the crucifixion begins. It pains God to lose us and it costs God to win us back.

Just before I went to college I read Helen Waddell's *Peter Abelard*. Abelard and his friend release a rabbit that is screaming from a snare. Abelard gathers up the little creature into his arms and there it dies. Abelard complains about the suffering and asks of God:

'Then why doesn't he stop it?'

'I don't know,' said Thibault. 'Unless – unless, it's like the Prodigal Son. I suppose the father could have kept him at home against his will. But what would have been the use? All this,' he stroked the limp body, 'is because of us. But all the time God suffers more than we do.'

Abelard looked at him perplexed . . .

'Thibault, do you mean Calvary?'

Thibault shook his head. 'That was only a piece of it – the piece that we saw – in time. Like that,' he pointed to a fallen tree beside them sawn through the middle, 'that dark ring there, it goes up and down the whole length of the tree. But we only see it where it is cut across. That is what Christ's life was; the bit of God that we saw. And we think God is like that, because Christ is like that, kind and forgiving sins and healing people. We think God is like that forever, because it happened once, with Christ. But not the pain. Not the agony at the last. We think that stopped.'

Abelard looked at him . . .

'Then Thibault,' he said slowly, 'you think that all this,' he looked at the quiet little body in his arms, 'all the pain of the world was Christ's cross?'

'God's cross,' said Thibault, 'and it goes on.'

(Waddell, 1945, pp. 288–91)

Though he had pained the love of his father, the Prodigal Son knew he could depend on that love. He felt that he could go home even if it was as the dispossessed son. He had lost his inheritance: he had wasted and not respected what was given to him. He was not worthy to be called a son. He had no rights, no claims on the father, except that he knew that the father loved him. He rehearsed in his mind what he would say. He would not seek privilege, he had no right to; he would ask to be taken back as a hired servant. To be like a hired servant in a loving household is better than being alone and starving to death. To be a hired servant is lower than being a slave, for a hired servant is only a day labourer and receives reward only on his output, he has to earn his living each day. This is not a world of grace but of reward for work done. In a good household a common slave was in a sense treated as a member of a family and given certain privileges. The hired servant could be dismissed at a day's notice; he was not a member of the family at all. The Prodigal was desperate and would come home on any terms. He would work for his keep; he would earn his place.

For many, this is the way they seek to return to God and his kingdom. True, we all come unworthy and dependent on grace. But there is a danger we come believing we can earn the kingdom like a day worker who earns his pay. There is still a belief that we can enter the kingdom only if we earn it. We believe it is only given like a star is given to a child for being good. We are slow to learn that God lavishes his love and offers us his kingdom freely. Nearly all of us want to earn the kingdom, to make it ours by rights, to claim that we deserve it. But this is to fail to understand that it is God's gift to us: it is the gift of himself and his love. If only we would come to our senses we would realize that we are already there, for we are offered the kingdom. This is expressed well in an affirmation from the Hebrides:

> I find thee enthroned in my heart, my Lord Jesus. I know
> that thou art throned in Heaven.
> My heart and Heaven are one.
>
> (Maclean, 1937, p. 106)

Too many people find this hard to accept. Like the Jews we think that God calls for a 'bank balance' of good deeds. There is still an image of the last day as when we are faced with a balance book with the credits of good deeds and the debits of bad deeds. Where the failure to live up to who we are comes into this I am not sure. If we are in credit with good deeds God has to let us in for we have earned it. If we are in a deficit due to bad deeds we will not gain the kingdom. Once again we cannot see that we can never earn the love of God or entrance to the kingdom. They are offered to us freely; we have to turn towards them and accept them. Once we turn, God is there waiting to meet us.

Though we may have moved far away, we can still be closer to loved ones than to those who are standing next to us. Separation is not just about distance; it is also about attitude. People can share the same room yet live totally separate lives. You can sit next to a stranger on a train but because of love you are nearer to your dear one who is miles away. The God who transcends all our ability to fully understand him is not spatially separated from us, but is close at hand. Transcendence does not describe separation, for if we were truly separated we would die. Transcendence describes his being beyond our comprehension but not beyond our experience and not beyond his love. In fact God is encountered daily in and through his creation, if we would only open ourselves to the reality of his loving presence and his kingdom. God is with us at every moment of our life. His kingdom is always there being freely offered, if only we would turn our attention, our life, in that direction. Our God ever seeks to meet us and have an encounter with us.

We must be careful not to replace our meeting with God by just thinking nice thoughts about him. Prayer is essentially standing before God with undivided attention, undivided in heart, undivided in mind, undivided in spirit. Prayer is seeking to restore a mutual relationship that we have broken by turning away. This is very difficult for us in an age when we are not encouraged to focus for long on anything. This is why I try to teach children to focus their attention on single things rather than flit from one thing to another. Perhaps I took to heart the words of Brother Lawrence that I read when I was in my teens:

> One way to recall easily the mind in the time of prayer, and preserve it more in rest, is not to let it wander too far at other times. You should keep it strictly in the Presence of God; and being accustomed to think of him often from time to time, you will find it easy to keep your mind calm at the time of prayer, or at least recall it from its wander-ings.                                   (Brother Lawrence, 1906, p. 47)

The power of recollection is often very poor today and people come to each other with divided attention. In the home the television can often be on and people only half-listen to each other. While someone is talking it is too easy to let the mind wander and to focus on other things. If this is the way we deal with each other then we are not likely to give our undivided attention to God. Yet God is there amid all the distractions, waiting to give himself to us.

There is an amazing scene offered as the son turns home: the father runs to meet him. He does not wait until the son turns up. He has been waiting for this moment and hurries towards his son. In a country where men wore long robes and did not find it easy or dignified to run this is an extraordinary act. The father actually ran to meet the son. He did not wait until the wretch came and threw himself at his feet. The father sees him when he is still a long way off and he runs to meet him and throws his arms around him. Those who found offence in the telling of the father's generosity at the beginning would find this image of the father running equally disturbing. The son returns dirty and in rags but the father hugs him and kisses him. How many have discovered this love in their parents, that they are accepted and forgiven regardless of the past? The father enfolds the son in his love and expresses his care for him. There is no judgement – only loving acceptance, a welcome home. There is no raking up the past – only joy that the son has returned. It is amazing how many cannot countenance such love, refuse to accept such love, a love that is freely given and does not count the cost.

The son begins to recite the words he has rehearsed, 'Father, I have sinned against heaven and before you; I am no longer worthy to be called your son.' The son is desperate and is willing to crawl back, though at the back of his mind somewhere he knew of the love of the father. The son would come back on any terms, for with the father he finds a fulfilment of his own being; he moves from loneliness and starvation into a much richer life. It is strange how many feel they need to grovel before God and forever proclaim their unworthiness. So much of the Church is caught up in concentrating on sin and suffering and has a theology that seems to centre on the cross. So few can accept the joy of the resurrection and the love that is offered.

The father expresses his delight in having his son back again. He does not let the son offer to be a hired servant. These words are not said for this is a welcome home, a loving acceptance. The father still wants his son back as a son and not as a hired man or a slave. His son has come back freely and he wants him to be free. The father gives orders that the best robe in the house should be brought and put on his son, a ring on his finger and shoes on his feet. There are no recriminations, only rejoicing. There is no holding back of love or generosity. All of the garments in the story have a meaning. The robe stands for being reinstated and with honour. The son is clothed with dignity once more. Some have suggested that this robe was what the son had left behind when he left home. It was something the father kept for it was his son's and his alone. The robe is an expression of love and belonging. Time and again Jesus suggested there is a place that is uniquely ours in the kingdom of God; only we can fill it but we have to choose to do so.

The ring is a symbol of authority; the son comes back not as a slave but as one who has the freedom of the household, the freedom of the estate. If a man gave another a ring it was like giving him the power of attorney. In the Old Testament we hear of Joseph being given a ring by Pharaoh and arrayed in new clothes (Genesis 41.42), and of Mordecai being given authority and power by being given the ring of King Ahasuerus (Esther 8.2, 8). When rings are given and exchanged in marriage it is a symbol of our giving our whole life to the other person who is before us. We are saying, 'Everything I have, everything I am is yours without reserve.' When we say 'my husband', 'my wife', 'my family', it does not mean that we possess them but rather that we give ourselves to them without reserve. Likewise when we talk of 'my God' we are talking about our wholehearted commitment to him. Yet at the same time the Father offers himself and his kingdom to each of us.

The shoes are signs of being a member of the family; slaves were not shod. The slave's dream in the spiritual song is of the time when 'all God's chillun got shoes'. The love and generosity of all these acts must have been amazing to those who heard of them. Love as lavish as this reveals how deep is the father's love. This is the sort of home any sensible person would like to belong to.

The father then asks for the fatted calf to be killed; this is to be a feast, a festival day. It is to be a time of rejoicing and celebrating for it is about the resurrection, about newness of life. Homecoming is a moving away from a life of loneliness and of self-centredness to a life enfolded in love and a life of rejoicing.

Whenever we make this discovery or take this turn in our lives we experience a resurrection. Susan Hill captures this feeling of new life in describing one of her characters in her book *Air and Angels*:

All of his past, the old interests and concern, dropped quite away from him, and his old self was sloughed off, like the skin. And looking about him he saw the world recreated, all things were strange but new, brave and infinitely rare and beautiful to his eyes. He looked at the sea and sky, at the stone beneath his feet, and the shimmer on the far horizon, and the bird balanced on the post ahead, and he knew he had never seen their like before, all were miraculously new to him. (Hill, 1991, p. 263)

But to come to that change we have to be willing to change our direction and at least admit to ourselves that we have to this point taken a wrong direction and need to turn around. Sometimes what we call repentance is actually a coming to ourself and realizing how below par we are living and how much better life could be if we did not spend so much time in trivial and passing things. We may suddenly realize that commitment to a cause or a person and giving of ourself is far more enriching than saying, 'Give me'. For this reason the resurrection experience is often associated with the discovery of being loved and wanting to love.

There is great delight shown by the father at the return of his son and he throws a party. Again and again we need reminding that it is a great joy to be part of the kingdom. The stories that are grouped in Luke 15 are all about joy in heaven and the stories were told because the scribes and Pharisees were grumbling that Jesus was welcoming and eating with sinners. It is sad that the Church often projects a miserable and censorious image of life when it should be proclaiming the resurrection and joy. We should show by the way we live the joy of being loved by God and living in his kingdom.

Though the parables in Luke 15 do not start with the words, 'the kingdom of God is like . . .' they are all parables of the kingdom and of a return to it. There is a different interesting thought in each parable. The sheep went astray through its own foolishness. It did not think about what it was doing and just wandered off. Sheep and people often believe the grass is sweeter and greener somewhere else. Many a person did not mean to end up where they did but they just did not think. They had nothing against God or even the Church; they just wandered away. Some would argue that a single stupid sheep was not worth the shepherd's bother when he had another 99. Yet every single one is precious to the shepherd, every one is unique and not just a number. He seeks for the sheep until he finds it; notice that he does not give up. It could be argued that he gives it more attention than it is worth. This love does not count the cost but, as Jesus would say elsewhere, 'The Good Shepherd lays down his life for the sheep.' This is a sheep that has a special relationship with the shepherd for he lifts it up and carries it on his shoulders. See how the shepherd is joyful in finding it and how he asks others to share in his joy (Luke 15.6). Then Jesus says, 'There will be more joy in heaven over one sinner who repents than over ninety-nine righteous people who need no repentance' (Luke 15.7). It would seem the joy of heaven and the censoriousness of the self-righteous are far apart. God's love and God's kingdom are not exclusive and if we seek to keep others out we exclude ourselves from the joy that is offered to us.

A friend of mine who is an artist painted Jesus carrying on his shoulders not a lamb but an old wayward sheep. It had lost half of its fleece and looked decidedly tatty; it was not an object of beauty. He depicted Jesus as weighed down by the sheep and with scratched and dirty hands. When I asked him about this painting he said that we too often portray Jesus with a nice cuddly lamb.

> Lambs do not often stray from their mothers; they stay close and under her protection. I wanted to show an old awkward ewe that had a tendency to break through fences and cause trouble with neighbours. The sort that some farmers would feel like sending to the butcher's! For me this is a better expression of how far God, Jesus, goes in his love.

I knew exactly what he meant and I felt he well portrayed how far God will go to find us and in his love seek to bring us home.

The coin got lost through no fault of its own, but by the carelessness or disregard of someone. There is a sense in which it just became detached. We may belong to a country or a family that feels it has no need for the hypothesis that is God. We may have grown up to a so-called secular society where any reference to God is frowned upon or where the Church is forever being done down by the press. But this does not mean that God has stopped seeking us through our experiences, through beauty and through the example of others. If we keep ourselves sensitive to what is around us, God's love and his kingdom will seek entry into our lives.

> Just when we are safest, there's a sunset touch,
> A fancy from a flower bell, someone's death,
> A chorus-ending from Euripides –
> And that's enough for fifty hopes and fears
> As old and new at once as nature's self,
> To rap and knock and enter in our soul.
> (Robert Browning, 1812–89)

God is a God who is forever seeking us and wanting to reveal his kingdom to us and so bestow his love upon us, as love is the true meaning of our life. It is thought that the coin might have been part of a headdress and even represented a dowry. To lose the coin would be like someone losing their wedding ring. I can remember a visitor to Holy Island in the churchyard among the grass. The tide was coming in and she had a bus to catch but she swore she would not leave the island until she found her ring. She openly said it was of little value to anyone else but to her it was precious. She would not want to replace it with another because it was special to her. 'I will stay here seeking until I find it.' Fortunately I had a metal detector at home and was able to assist in the search and very soon the detector found it in some long grass. The delight on the woman's face was wonderful. For a moment I got a glimpse of the joy in heaven over a lost person who returns to God.

When the son is welcomed home there are no accusations, no recriminations – only joy, a joy that is meant to be shared in a relationship of mutual love.

## Exercises

1 Thoughts

> The Trinity is God, and God is the Trinity.
> The Trinity is our maker and keeper.
> The Trinity is our everlasting lover, our joy and our
>     bliss, through our Lord Jesus Christ.
>
> He is our clothing. In his love he wraps and holds us.
> He enfolds us for love, and he will never let us go.
> I saw that he is to us everything that is good.
>
> (Julian of Norwich, quoted in
> *Enfolded in Love*, 1980, p. 1)

God is properly called love because he is the cause of all love and is poured through all things and gathers all things into one and returns to himself in an unutterable way and brings to an end in himself the loves of every creature.　　　(John Scotus Erigena, *c.* 810–77)

2　Read the parable of the two debtors in Matthew 18.21–35.

**Pause, Presence, Picture, Ponder, Promise**

**Pause**　Stop all that you are doing. Know that you do not need to justify your life by perpetual action. Be still and let the love and peace of God flow into you as you let the sun shine upon you. Make space in your daily routine for this to happen. Enter the stillness, seek to relax your body and your mind, breathe deeply and slowly and seek to rest.

**Presence**　Rejoice in the presence and love of God. Know that the Creator of all loves you and that God is with you now. Try to do without words, just enjoy being in God's presence and love. If you need words use a short sentence that affirms the presence. You may like to say:

You, Lord, are with me,
always with me.
You, Lord, love me,
always love me.

**Picture**　Peter coming to Jesus and seeking what we would now call damage limitation. He felt that forgiveness needed to have some limits. The Jewish teaching was quite simple: if someone sins forgive them, once, twice, three times but after that enough is enough. A sinner must be made to face consequences. Some would even suggest that God forgave only up to three times and would cite the early chapters of Amos, where nations are punished on the fourth transgression. That is sensible enough and kind enough. Peter saw that Jesus was going beyond this and asked how often he should forgive, until seven times? Surely this was as much as anyone could do; it was more than most thought God would go! Jesus refused to put a limit on forgiveness and suggested 70 times seven; in other words, without limit. Love and forgiveness cannot start setting limits.

Visualize the story about two debtors with whom the king wished to settle accounts. One was brought owing ten thousand talents. This is a ridiculous amount of money; it was greater than a king's ransom. It was more money than the revenue from all of Samaria and Galilee put together. It was an amount no one could pay. Yet the king forgives him this debt out of love, out of care for the man's wife and children.

This man, forgiven such an enormous debt, attacked a fellow-slave who owed him a hundred denarii – the sort of money that could be carried easily in a pocket. He was not merciful; he was not forgiving. He had the slave put into prison for his debt. He was a hard man. He demanded what was his by rights – and he had a right to. Fellow slaves were distressed by this and reported it to the king. The king was very angry and had the unforgiving slave put in prison until he could pay the debt – would he ever?

**Ponder**    This story tells us of the deep and costly love of God but also of the danger of an unforgiving heart. The unforgiving heart is damning. Hatred, vengeance, resentment can all poison our lives. God would forgive but cannot forgive the unforgiving. It seems forgiveness cannot be poured in if forgiveness is not given out. As we receive so we must give.

Forgiveness, like love, grows only by our giving it out. We cannot claim forgiveness if we are unwilling to forgive others. We cannot seek acceptance from God if we are excluding people from love and forgiveness. We must all pray the Lord's Prayer with caution when we say, 'Forgive us . . . as we forgive.'

**Promise**   to seek to forgive as you are forgiven and to love as you are loved. Remember, when you pour love and forgiveness out God is able to pour them into you.

3  Pray

> O God of love, we ask you to give us love;
> Love in our thinking, love in our speaking,
> Love in our doing,
> And love in the hidden places of our souls;
> Love of those with whom we find it hard to bear,
> And love of those who find it hard to bear with us;
> Love of those with whom we work,
> And love of those with whom we take our ease;
> So that at length we may be worthy to dwell with you,
> Who are eternal love.
>
> (William Temple, 1881–1944,
> quoted in Ashwin, 1996, p. 35)

# Not at Home at Home

Those who heard Jesus tell the story of the return of the Prodigal Son would not have found it easily acceptable. Surely the son deserved to pay the price for his wandering? How could the father so readily accept him back into the family? In the balancing of the book of life the good should get rewarded and the not-so-good or the bad should pay for their wrong. Though they may have thought of how Israel was welcomed back to the Promised Land after exile in Babylon, there was a certain reasoning that suggested they were welcome back because they deserved it more than the nations around them. Most had still to learn that they were redeemed by God's love and not their own worth. Jesus in his ministry went out to the outcasts and sinners; he sought out like a good shepherd those who had got lost and wandered afar off. The scribes and Pharisees thought that in many ways such people were a waste of time and would only contaminate the faith. They thought,

> If you welcome rogues and vagabonds, if you mix with tax-gatherers and sinners, are you not in danger of weakening the law and becoming soft in your dealings? Are you not also in danger of being contaminated by them? Does not God love us for we have earned his love? Any who do not earn that love deserve to be on the outside.

This reasoning is still common today and there are many groups that seek to make God's love exclusive rather than inclusive.

Those who seek to keep God to themselves and their way of thinking and who refuse to see that God welcomes all to his love and his kingdom cause many acts of violence. Sadly they often do this 'in the name of God'. This is truly taking God's name in vain.

There would be a definite feeling among the Scribes and Pharisees that Jesus was getting at them when he talked of the older son. The Jews had known the true God longer than any other nation and they did not want others coming in and taking their inheritance. It was hard to accept that the love of God was for all, even those who had worked but 'one hour', when they had laboured so long to keep the faith. How could sinners and Gentiles be welcomed on the same footing? There is still the desire to go back to earning the kingdom and the love of God and not accepting that they are freely offered to all. In a strange way when we seek to restrict God's love we fail to enjoy that love ourselves, for we have diminished the love offered.

The one who was entitled to all that was left, the older brother, is sorry that his brother has come home. He does not even talk of 'my brother' but only of 'this son of yours', and there is meant to be a sting in the words. There is the sense that the older brother wants nothing to do with his younger brother and so has disowned him. It is always easier to condemn someone if we separate ourselves from them, and have no love towards them. When Cain killed Abel he refused to acknowledge any responsibility for his brother (Genesis 4.9). This separation does not just injure our brother or sister; it injures us and creates division not only between peoples but also between us and God. The atonement is about breaking down these divisions.

I once knew a family that had many problems. Today they would be described as a dysfunctional family. The father was very domineering and unforgiving. The two teenage children were rebellious and forever getting into trouble. The mother strove to keep peace in a troubled household. Whenever the father was annoyed or upset by his teenage children he railed at his wife, saying: 'Have you seen what your son has done now?' or 'Do you know what your daughter has done?' There was a sense in which he disowned them. He had cast them off: they were nothing to do with him. Often after such a statement he would impose a punishment that was in fact to hurt all of them. Later in life he would boast of his daughter who was a doctor and of his son who was doing well in business. When they had earned it he claimed them as his, though he then ignored the great rift he had caused in his family.

In the story of the Prodigal Son, the older brother enters the scene like the demon king in the pantomime. We are hearing of redeeming love, of resurrection, of forgiveness, acceptance and celebration; then enters the shadow, the accuser. If he can, he will put a stop to all this idea of undeserved love and an easy return to the father. The older brother could stand on his rights; he could invoke the law, for the younger brother had wasted his share.

He accuses the Prodigal by saying, 'This son of yours . . . who devoured your property with prostitutes.' How does he know? He was not there. He wants to throw a bit of mud about. It is amazing how many people like to throw around accusations and slurs on a character. In the book of Revelation the devil is described as 'the accuser of our comrades'. But the accuser has been conquered for 'now have come the salvation and the power and the kingdom of our God and the authority of his Messiah' (Revelation 12.10). God forgives; the devil accuses: God brings together in atonement; the devil is known as *diabolos* for he is the one who divides and throws apart. The separation of heaven from earth, of matter from spirit, of God from us is all of the devil. Anyone who refuses to forgive and goes around accusing people sides not with God but with the forces of evil. In the kingdom of heaven there are no accusations but only acceptance and forgiveness. But these gifts are from the grace of God and can be given to us only if we reflect them in our lives.

The older son reminds me of the servant in a Brontë novel who took all the blessings upon himself and gave all the curses out to others. There was a rule for himself and yet another rule for other people. Once again, it is amazing how many people can excuse themselves but not others. Some would count themselves God's favourites to the extent of excluding others from the same love. To be an accuser, to be unloving and unforgiving, is to choose to step outside of the kingdom of God. The older son could not see any good or beauty for he lived not in the freedom of love but under the law. This son reminds me of the man with the muck rake in *Pilgrim's Progress*: 'A man that could look no ways but downwards, with a muck rake in his hand.'

There is no desire to enter into the celebration, to share in the forgiveness, no desire to rejoice with his father. The older son cannot come into the presence and cannot enter into the joy.

This man alienates himself and refuses to come in. His attitude to his father is interesting in that it shows his years of obedience are out of duty, under the law and not of grace. He has not discovered the service which is perfect freedom. He has failed to see that the relationship with the father is of the heart; not duty but love. He has kept the rules but has not discovered a loving father; he has been a son in outward things only. God wants love more than sacrifice or slavish service. Yet many a son and daughter cannot enjoy the kingdom of God because they live with the God of Mount Sinai and can only approach him with rules and regulations, and they will not allow others to approach him except through the rule book. Sadly this is what keeps many 'good' people from entering into the joys of the kingdom.

At the same time there is a desire to make the father take notice of him by his attitude. There is a lot of emotion here; there is anger, resentment and probably a good deal of jealousy. How often we come up against situations like this in families. How many have been hurt by the self-righteous attitude or the jealousy of a sibling? The rebellious rage of those who feel as if they are slaves is always in danger of exploding. I know many a 'righteous' person who is like an unexploded bomb, for inside are resentments and jealousies that are ready to burst out at any moment.

'I have never disobeyed a single command of yours.' The older son measures by obedience and transgressions. This is how the Pharisees measured. St Paul in his letter to the Philippians describes himself as a Pharisee and 'as to righteousness under the law, blameless'. He goes on to say how this attitude is nothing compared with the surpassing value of 'knowing Christ', which is having a living, loving relationship with him. More than righteousness Paul declares: 'I want to know Christ and the power of his resurrection' (Philippians 3.6, 10). This is the relationship the Pharisees and many others were denying themselves because of their attitude to Jesus and to God.

This son declares his obedience but he is actually refusing at this very moment to do what the father was asking of him. If he is refusing to do now what the father asks, can you really believe it is the first act of disobedience? Here is a man not at home in his father's house and – worse – many count him as religious. I always fear those who are not at home in this world, for they send out signals of discontent and dissatisfaction. They remind me of Matthew Arnold's words:

# Living in Two Kingdoms

> Wandering between two worlds, one dead
> The other powerless to be born
> With nowhere yet to rest my head,
> Like these, on earth I wait forlorn.
>
> (Matthew Arnold, 1822–88,
> from 'Stanzas from the Grande Chartreuse')

To not be at home in this world is a slight on its Creator. To divide heaven from earth is to give way to dualism. To live just an earthly existence is to give way to materialism. In the Christian faith we seek to show a dialectic at work where spirit and matter are inseparable, where heaven and earth are one in a living and ever-changing relationship. In this we witness to the fact that we dwell in God and he in us. We are at home with God and he is at home in our homes.

The story ends with the older son in a rage and deliberately disobeying the father. We see that the father comes out to him but he refuses to come to the celebration. Though he has his own rituals it would seem that life is not a celebration for him and he cannot accept the broadness of the father's love. He finds that love beyond his comprehension. Frederick William Faber captured this attitude in his hymn 'There's a wideness in God's mercy':

> For the love of God is broader
> than the measures of man's mind
> and the heart of the Eternal
> is most wonderfully kind.
>
> But we make his love too narrow
> by false limits of our own;
> and we magnify his strictness
> with a zeal he will not own.
>
> (Frederick William Faber, 1814–63)

If we are the chosen people it is not because God wants to keep the others out; rather we have been chosen to bring the others in. By our attitude to the world, to others, to life, we should reveal the delight God has in all of his creation and the love he offers to it. We should show the need to celebrate every day the mystery of God's love and his coming to us in the world. There is always something to celebrate when anyone turns from darkness to light, from hunger to a celebration, when people turn from being self-centred and move towards the other. We should see this in terms of resurrection, a rising to newness of life, of living in the kingdom of heaven.

When the father is delighting in his world, when his brother is experiencing newness of life, a loving brother would rejoice. But here is a grumbler and a complainer. It is a refusal to see love at work. It is the tendency to look at mud when we are offered stars. The father has 'welcome home' written on his heart – but this son refuses to come in. Jealousy and anger are no strangers to family life or to the Church. Again the hearers would say the father should have left him outside to starve; it would not be long before he was pleading to come in. But notice the father comes out to where he is. We may exclude ourselves from God but he does not exclude us from his presence and love.

Jesus wanted his hearers to relate the story to their lives. What he is talking about is happening here and now. The elder son, in many ways, represents the people of Israel, who were brought out of captivity with great celebration but now have not only created an exclusive God but also made a life of freedom into one of rules and regulations. The obedience offered is not so much of love but of fear; it is far from the 'perfect freedom' which God offers. There are many pseudo-values offered to all of us; they come in forms that make them look good – religious dogmatism, legalism, consumerism, even imperialism, are presented as virtues. The danger of the fundamentalist is not just what he believes but his insistence that you must conform. One of the greatest weapons of control freaks is the law book, whether it is the Ten Commandments or some book of human rules.

Jesus had come to bring them out of this captivity, to help them return to the fullness of life and to learn that life is to be celebrated. He came to reveal that the love of God is not limited but is open to all; it is not for Jews only but for the rest of the world also. This should be cause for real celebration. Jesus was aware of the anger that this was causing and how God's own people were keeping themselves outside this love by their attitude. They could not enter into the joy of life and were put out when others seemed able to do it. The Church has often come across as a killjoy.

In some ways Jesus would seek to show that this was not new teaching. The story of Jonah, which is meant to be the story of Israel, is about someone asked to go one way by God who goes the opposite way. He had been asked to help Nineveh to repent but sets off in the other direction in protest. But going against the grain in the world only causes trouble for ourselves and others. Jonah and his companions are caught in a storm. Only by casting Jonah overboard do the rest get any peace. Jonah enters into captivity, which is very like entering the kingdom of the dead. If he stays there, he will die. But he is set free and seeks to go in the direction he was asked. There is never a suggestion that this is an easy road. Jonah is provided with shelter from the heat. When his shelter dies, he is angry. He is angry at the death of a plant. Should he not care in the same way for the people of Nineveh and all that are in it? This is a story to make the people who were brought out of captivity think of God's mission of love and redemption being offered to others. Too often after leaving captivity, people hold on to a desert mentality.

They fail to enter or to rejoice in the Promised Land; that is, they are not truly at home in God's world.

## Exercises

1 Thoughts

> Not everyone who says to me, 'Lord, Lord', will enter the kingdom of heaven, but only one who does the will of my Father in heaven. (Matthew 7.21)

It is not just what we profess with our lips, it is the way we live that shows that we are part of God's kingdom. In the story of the Prodigal Son it is the older 'righteous' son who ends up with his back turned to his father.

> By love alone is God enjoyed, by love alone delighted in, by love alone approached and admired. His nature requires this. The law of nature commands thee to love him: the law of his nature and the law of thine.
>
> (Thomas Traherne, 1636–74,
> from 'Centuries of Meditations')

2 Read the parable of the two sons in Matthew 21.28–31.

**Pause, Presence, Picture, Ponder, Promise**

**Pause**  Take time out to delight in the fact that you are God's creation and in God's world. You do not have to earn this; you are asked to delight in it. Let go all tension from your body – do a check over each part. Relax. Still the mind and its need to achieve. If you need words to enter into the silence you may like to say:

Drop thy still dews of quietness,
till all our strivings cease;
take from our souls the strain and stress,
and let our ordered lives confess
the beauty of thy peace.

(John Greenleaf Whittier, 1807–92,
from 'The Brewing of Soma')

**Presence**   Know that God is with you. You do not have to make efforts to reach him: he comes to where you are. Learn the truth of the text 'Draw near to God, and he will draw near to you' (James 4.8).

Quietly affirm the Presence. Know that God is always with you. If you feel you have lost your grip on God, know that he has a firm hold on you.

**Picture**   Jesus in the Temple, and facing the chief priests and elders. These were the people who should be showing others how to love and serve God. They had been given a wonderful inheritance with the Scriptures, the Temple and all their traditions. They had a relationship with the Father. Jesus sees that they are failing to reach out in the love of God. He tells them a parable about two sons. This is a little parable that does not set out to praise anyone for it shows a far from ideal situation. Neither of these two sons could really bring joy to the father. These two young men look like part of a dysfunctional family. The father asks the first to go and work in the vineyard and he simply replies, 'No, I will not.' And off he goes; he is free to go and the father does not force him. The father goes to the second son and asks the same. This time he gets a better reply: 'Yes, sir, I will go.' It sounds good, but he does not bother; he does not go and work in the vineyard. Fortunately the first son has a change of heart and goes to work in the vineyard. It is easy to know which one did the will of the father – and he did it out of love.

**Ponder**   Think how there are people who make a great show of their piety, of their religion, but who fail to show it in their daily lives. They may have all the right words and speak to please but in their hearts and wills they fail to live up to what they promise. Fine words are no substitute for deeds. We show our love by what we do far more than by what we say. Many people fail to do what they say. On this level I wonder how anyone can say they actually believe in God and then not bother to get to know him.

There is a large group of people who would call themselves non-church people; they may call themselves materialists but their actions of love and acceptance show them to be nearer to working with God than some of the hardhearted legalists. To hear Jesus say, 'Tax-collectors and prostitutes are going into the kingdom of God ahead of you' should really make us stop and think. Jesus was not implying that every tax-collector and prostitute was finding their way into the kingdom. But he was showing that they were able to react and to turn towards the ways of God. Think over the truth that where love is, God is.

**Promise**   to seek to show each day that you are in God's kingdom by seeking to rejoice in his Presence and to help to reveal his love to others.

3   Pray

> O God our Leader and our Master and our Friend,
> forgive our imperfections and our little motives,

take us and make us one with thy great purpose,
use us and do not reject us,
make us all servants of thy kingdom,
weave our lives into thy struggle to conquer and to
    bring peace and union to the world.
We are small and feeble creatures,
we are feeble in speech, feebler still in action,
nevertheless let thy light shine upon us,
and there is not one of us that cannot be lit by thy fire
and who cannot lose himself in thy salvation.
Take us into thy purposes, O God,
let thy kingdom come into our hearts and into the
    world.

(H. G. Wells, 1866–1946,
from 'To Declare to the Father')

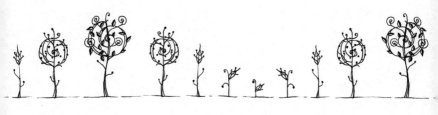

# Alive Again

In a Gospel that is about the resurrection we cannot overlook the statement made twice by the father of the Prodigal Son: 'This son of mine was dead and is alive again; he was lost and is found!' (Luke 15.24) and 'This brother of yours was dead and has come to life; he was lost and has been found' (Luke 15.32). I would like to add the words of the Prodigal earlier in the story when he says, 'I will arise and go to my father' (Luke 15.18, AV); the New Revised Standard Version misses the impact of the words in just having, 'I will get up'. In turning to the father the resurrection begins, the opportunity for newness of life is offered. In turning to the father there is a moving away from captivity and death.

I feel that throughout the Gospels there are suggestions of resurrection which are often 'lost in translation'. The following are examples where the Authorized Version uses the word 'arise' and the New Revised Standard Version only has 'stand up' or something similar:

- It may not be obvious among all the wealth he was collecting but Matthew was not much better off than the Prodigal Son. Matthew had become a collaborator with the enemy of occupation. He was a son of Levi so was of the priestly family. But by his actions he had become banned from worship with his people. When he arose and followed Jesus there is no doubt that for Matthew the resurrection was already at

95

work (Matthew 9.9; Mark 2.14). It may be of no coincidence that Matthew's Gospel places this call between two other 'resurrections': the paralysed man is commanded to arise (Matthew 9.5–6; Mark 2.9, 11–12; Luke 5.24) and later in the same chapter there is the dead girl whom Jesus took by the hand and the maid arose (Matthew 9.25; cf. Mark 5.41–42; Luke 8.54–55).

- Mark tells of a boy who apparently has some form of epileptic fit. The boy fell down and was like a corpse before Jesus. Most of those who were there said, 'He is dead.' Jesus took him by the hand and lifted him up and he arose (Mark 9.27).
- Luke tells the story of a dead man who was the only son of a widow at Nain. The dead man was being carried out for his burial. Jesus the Lord of life stopped the funeral procession. He touched the bier and said to the young man, 'Arise' (Luke 7.14). Life was restored to him and he was given back to his mother.
- In the story of the Prodigal Son we are told he said, 'I will arise and go to my father' and that 'he arose' (Luke 15.18, 20, AV).
- When Jesus was in the region between Samaria and Galilee ten lepers approached him. Because of their disease, lepers were not only banned from normal life but also not allowed to make contact with healthy people, and they were counted as already dead. When one of the ten returned to give thanks to Jesus for his healing and prostrated himself at the feet of Jesus, Jesus said, 'Arise, go thy way: thy faith hath made thee whole' (Luke 17.19, AV). Once again there is little doubt that, for this man, a resurrection experience took place.

Time and again we are given the opportunity for newness of life. Through the love of God we are able to experience a rising from what would keep us in captivity and to enter the glorious freedom of children of God. With St Patrick I want to say, 'I arise today.'

> I arise today
> Through the mighty strength, the invocation of the
>     Trinity,
> Through belief in the threeness,
> Through confession of the oneness
> Of the Creator of Creation.
>
> I arise today
> Through the strength of Christ's birth with His baptism,
> Through the strength of His crucifixion with His burial,
> Through the strength of His resurrection with His
>     ascension,
> Through the strength of His descent for the judgement
>     of doom.
> I arise today . . .
>
> (Meyer, 1928, p. 25)

Our resurrection is possible through the power and the love of God. Like the kingdom of God, it is a tragedy if we put the resurrection off to beyond the grave. It is a wonderful experience that will happen to us again and again. It is good to recognize our mini-resurrections and to give thanks to God for each of them. At the start of some days I like to use the words from John Keble:

> New every morning is the love
> our wakening and uprising prove;
> through sleep and darkness safely brought
> restored to life and power and thought.

New mercies each returning day,
hover around us when we pray;
new perils past, new sins forgiven,
new thoughts of God, new hopes of heaven.

(John Keble, 1792–1866)

There is more than this: I believe in the resurrection of the body. Though I am not fully sure of what this means I do believe it is concerned with my own uniqueness. I am not absorbed into the Godhead, nor lost in transformation. What survives is me; if I did not survive as myself then there is no resurrection of the body. To say the 'body' does not necessarily mean the material body that we have now but it does mean all that makes us who we are; it is our essential unique being.

I get much comfort from modern research into DNA and the emphasis on our uniqueness. Our birth is a wonderful mystery and would be beyond belief if we did not know it happens. We begin as a single fertilized cell, not discernible to the human eye. That cell is given the ability to divide and divide again and again. By the time you have become an adult the one will have become 50 trillion cells, each one with its programme to keep you healthy and alive. You have 100 million sense cells in each of your eyes alone. Every cell is like a great instruction book and carries the entire instructions of about 100,000 genes. Every moment of the day your body is making new cells. A molecule of DNA splits itself in two by dividing down the centre; then out of the sea of chemicals it rebuilds itself to make two exact replicas of the original molecule. Though the DNA molecule appears to be made up of matter such as hydrogen, oxygen and carbon atoms it has something else within it that makes you uniquely you. It has an inbuilt programme for you and you alone. No one else in the whole universe has DNA like yours and that uniqueness is stamped on every molecule that is yours.

Your body is a wonderful mystery, unique to this world, and yet it is dying – and being reborn at the rate of millions of times every minute. In every single second, cells are dying and continue to be renewed. The body is going through a process of death and resurrection all the time. Your body has known millions of deaths and experienced millions of resurrections. If God has made this possible on a day-to-day level I do not doubt that he could give us the power to survive what we call death.

Sometimes as an exercise, when I can bear it, I take out my photograph album and look at the stages of my life, not only as infant, schoolboy, miner, student, priest and writer but also at all the experiences I have had and all the bodies I have worn out! There are stages when my body has gone through big changes, yet I am still here, and all the previous bodies are definitely mine. I have experienced more than a few deaths and resurrections. We do not stay long enough with the wonder and mystery of our own being to be thrilled by our existence. I am reminded of this as I read Augustine:

> Men go abroad to wonder at the height of mountains, at the huge waves of the sea, at the long courses of rivers, at the vast compass of the ocean, at the circular motion of the stars; and they pass by themselves without wondering.
> (Augustine, 354–430, from *The Confessions of St Augustine*, Book X)

If we cease to marvel at who we are, or take for granted the mysteries that are about us, how can we hope to be aware of the greater mystery of God as our Creator? Too often we go around as if we are sleepwalking and not alert to the mystery that is around us. We need to focus more and give our attention to the depths of our being and the wonder of this God-filled creation. Pierre Teilhard de Chardin expresses this well in his book, *Le Milieu Divin*:

> All around us, to right and left, in front and behind, above and below, we have only to go a little beyond the frontier of sensible appearances in order to see the divine welling up and showing through . . . By means of all created things without exception, the divine assails us, penetrates us, moulds us. We imagined it as distant and inaccessible, whereas in fact we live steeped in its burning layers. *In eo vivimus.* As Jacob said, awakening from his dream, the world, this palpable world, which we were wont to treat with boredom and disrespect with which we habitually regard places with no sacred association for us, is truly a holy place, and we did not know it. *Venite adoremus.*

> (Pierre Teilhard de Chardin, 1881–1955)

The Celtic wing of the Church was often criticized for not making much mention of the resurrection. They erected many crosses and often mentioned the cross but there are not many references to the resurrection. But this is a criticism of words, for the great emphasis of the Celtic Christians is the abiding presence of Father, Son and Holy Spirit. They talked to the risen Lord in a very ordinary day-to-day acknowledgement that he was with them. They had their Lord as a companion on the road and when they went fishing just as the disciples did of old. He was their friend and fellow traveller and so there was little need to look back towards the tomb. Talking and singing to the living Lord gave strength and glory to their day. They spoke to the Lord in the morning at fire-lighting, in their work, as they walked and as they lay down to sleep. He was a constant companion at their side. Christ is not a figure of history but to be met, for he is the risen Lord.

Saviour and friend, how wonderful art thou!
My companion on the changeful way.
The comforter of its weariness.
My guide to the eternal town
The welcome at its gate.

(Maclean, 1937, p. 25)

The Celtic crosses are anything but empty. They are usually filled with intricate knotwork patterns. It is thought that the Celtic high crosses were usually painted in bright colours. This makes me think of Easter Day on Holy Island when four or five full-sized crosses are carried into church. Pilgrims have come from all over the North of England and the border of Scotland carrying these large crosses for a week as they walk towards Holy Island. These crosses will have been a heavy weight over many a moor and fell. Now on Easter Day the crosses are covered in spring flowers, symbols of life and love, signs of the resurrection. They are brought in as we sing with joy, for Christ is risen, Alleluia; he is risen indeed, Alleluia!

The Celtic knotwork patterns with their continual crossing, going under and rising, are seen as symbols of life and the resurrection in the way the line goes under and then rises continually. Throughout our lives we go under but we rise again. The other feature of the knotwork patterns is that they are endless: they are a symbol of eternity. Stamped on nearly every Celtic cross is this symbol of eternity.

The Celtic Christians sought to make the resurrection part of their own experience. At rising they would say prayers like the following:

Thanks to Thee, O God, that I have risen today,
To the rising of life itself;
May it be to Thine own glory, O God of every gift,
And to the glory of my soul likewise.

                                    (Carmichael, 1976, p. 31)

It is a pity that in the busyness of life many have lost the ability to recognize the Presence in their midst and the awareness that they can converse with the risen Lord. This is the only part of the gospel you truly can make your own. The whole of the gospel story is in a sense history; it is past and we can only enter it through using our imaginations and relating it to our lives. But the Christ is the risen Lord to be met and we can have a living relationship with him. The risen Lord is here and with each of us now! You can relate to him or ignore him – the choice is yours. It is of little value talking about the resurrection if we do not seek to be aware of it in our lives and to relate to the risen Christ. St Symeon the New Theologian said: 'How can one who knows nothing of the resurrection in this life expect to discover it and enjoy it in his death?' These are strong words indeed.

St Paul, who experienced a resurrection of his own on the Damascus road when he met the living Lord, said: 'If Christ has not been raised, your faith is futile and you are still in your sins' (1 Corinthians 15.17). St John, who uses the term 'eternal life' for 'heaven', tells us that in the love of God we are not perishable goods: 'God so loved the world that he gave his only Son, so that everyone who believes in him may not perish but may have eternal life' (John 3.16). The belief that St John calls for is not a set of credal statements but an invitation to have a personal relationship with God and with the risen Lord.

Only the resurrection and the awareness that life is eternal can make this world, which is often dark and cruel, a place of light and hope. Only the knowledge that God welcomes us to be with him each day can make us truly at home in this world and able to say that 'death is not fatal'! We cannot put off the kingdom of God or the resurrection until when we die, though we will experience them then in a deeper and more wonderful way. We must be at home in and delight in God's kingdom now.

Though we celebrate the resurrection each year on the fixed day of Easter, we need to make it a daily celebration in our lives. God wants us to celebrate and enjoy the fact that we are already at home with him. You may like to use part of the Paschal Homily of John Chrysostom as a regular invitation to enjoy life with God and glory in newness of life:

> Let everyone who loves God rejoice in this festival of
> light!
> Let the faithful servant gladly enter the joy of his Lord!
> Let those who have borne the burden of fasting come
> now to reap their reward!
> Let those who have worked since the first hour receive
> now their just wage!
> Let those who came after the third hour keep this festival
> with gratitude!
> Let those who arrived only after the sixth hour, approach
> without fear:
> they will not be defrauded.
> If someone has come at the ninth hour, let him come
> without hesitation.
> And let not the worker at the eleventh hour be ashamed,
> the Lord is generous.
> He welcomes the last to come no less than the first.
> He welcomes into his peace the worker of the eleventh
> hour
> as kindly as he welcomes the one who has worked since
> dawn.

The first he fills to overflowing and on the last he has
  compassion.
To the one he grants his favour and to the other his pardon.
He does not look only on the work he sees but on the
  intention of the heart . . .
The table is laid: come all of you without misgivings.
The fatted calf is served, let all take their fill.
All of you share in the banquet of faith:
all of you draw on the wealth of his mercy.

(John Chrysostom, *c.* 347–407)

## Exercises

### 1 Thoughts

> How can one who knows nothing of the resurrection in
> this life expect to discover it and enjoy it in his death?
> (St Symeon the New Theologian, 949–1022)

God freely created us so that we might know, love and
serve him in this life and be happy with him forever.
God's purpose in creating us is to draw forth from us
a response of love and service here on earth, so that we
may obtain our goal of everlasting happiness with him
in heaven.

All things in this world are gifts of God, created for
us, to be the means by which we can come to know
him better, love him more surely and serve him more
faithfully.

As a result, we ought to appreciate and use these
gifts of God insofar as they help us towards our goal of
loving service and union with God. But insofar as any
created things hinder our progress toward our goal, we
ought to let them go.     (Ignatius Loyola, 1491–1556)

2 Read the parable of the seed growing secretly in Mark
4.26–29.

**Pause, Presence, Picture, Ponder, Promise**

**Pause** Stop all that you are doing and rest in the love and
peace of God as you would in the sunshine. There is no need
for effort – only to place yourself there. Relax in the knowledge that you are enfolded in his love. His peace is here. Let
it soothe a tense body. Check that you are relaxed from head
to foot and just stay there for a while.

**Presence** Affirm that you are at this moment and every
moment in the presence of God. There is no need to try and
make God come for he is there with you. Take to heart the
words of Scripture: 'Be still and know that I am God.' If the
mind wants to wander bring it back. If you need words to do
this, say, 'I am with God: God is with me.'

**Picture** the sowing of seeds in the ground. This in itself is
an act of faith, in the seed and in the seasons. You may want
to picture yourself preparing the ground, weeding, rooting
out, digging. Once the seed is sown you can go about your
daily work and you can sleep, though you know the ground
may need some attention and more weeding. You know that
if you plant the seed and give it the opportunity it will ger-
minate, it will grow. This is not of your doing; it is in the
ordering of the world. You can help it to grow but you do not
make it grow. There is a sense in which growth is automatic,
spontaneous. Even then it is not instant but gradual. There
are the first tender shoots – sometimes needing protection
from frosts. Then the blade, then the ear; growth is wonderful and often very abundant from a few small seeds. Finally

comes the harvest. See the field being cut and the grain gathered.

**Ponder**   This is what the kingdom of heaven is like and you are the ground; it is a germinal principle, a principle of growth: 'The kingdom is within you.' The same principle is at work in all the world. But the seed will only grow if you encourage it – if you make sure it is there. Then it will grow in ways you do not know, but it will grow. The danger is of you allowing weeds to choke it out or not allowing it enough depth for proper growth. But there is no doubt the kingdom of God is there, planted by God himself and waiting for you just to encourage and assist that growing in your life. This growth itself is a sign of the resurrection: that 'love is come again like grass that springeth green'. For those who know this secret growth and harvest, death is not the end, for we know that life and the kingdom go on.

**Promise**   to seek and to encourage the growth of God's rule of love, of the knowledge of his presence in your life. Spend a little time each day sowing seeds of the Presence and giving them the chance to grow.

3  Pray

> Though the dawn break cheerless on this Isle today,
> my spirit walks upon a path of light.
> For I know my greatness.
> Thou hast built me a throne within Thy heart.
> I dwell safely within the circle of Thy care.
> I cannot for a moment fall out of the everlasting arms.
> I am on my way to glory.

(Maclean, 1937, p. 55)

# The Valley of Delight

One of the desires of the Celtic monks was to 'find the place of their resurrection'. This was a place where they would fulfil their vocation and serve God faithfully until their death. Perhaps for some this call came when they found life was being lived on a lower level than they wanted or when all had become routine rather than love. I believe the place of resurrection they were hunting out was not a place to die in but instead was a place to live their life to the full, a place to extend themselves and a place where they could be aware of the love and the presence of God. There is no doubt they could have discovered this place anywhere; it was available to them wherever they were. But in their search there is a suggestion that there is a unique place for them not only in heaven but also on earth. There is the suggestion that we are all created for a purpose. We may feel that the world, which often appears to be far from God, hinders us in fulfilling our purpose. This may be true, for sin is often present in all the ways of the world. The world is far from perfect, as we know it. If we feel restricted or hindered we can at least turn towards God and that is the beginning of a resurrection. We can affirm that we belong to God no matter what is going on around us. We can rejoice that nothing will separate us from the love of God in Christ Jesus, not even death. We are not only children of the king; we are already in his kingdom. In this way no matter how bad the day or the events, we can in God make it a place of resurrection, a 'lifting place'.

The Quakers who emigrated to America and Canada did not talk of 'a place of resurrection' but used a phrase in one of their hymns that I find deeply meaningful. They hoped to build a new life in a new world. They would face many challenges and often death but they rejoiced in God and in his presence as they often sang in the Appalachian mountains:

> It's a gift to be simple,
> It's a gift to be free,
> It's a gift to come down where we ought to be,
> And when we see ourselves in a way that's right,
> We will live in a valley of love and delight.

This world can be a vale of sorrows, there is much in this world that is far from the loving rule of God, but like pioneers we are able to seek to usher in the kingdom of God. In God and in forwarding his kingdom we seek to transform wherever we can the vale of sorrows into the valley of delight. We are to delight in God's world and his presence within it and to encourage others to do the same. This will often call for the gift of simplicity, the willingness not to dominate or possess. It will call us to reveal the glorious freedom that belongs to children of God. We are not bound by the fates and not even by death. We can show in our lives that 'death is conquered; we are free: Christ has won the victory'. In the words of St Augustine we can show that 'we are resurrection people and Alleluia is our song'.

There is an affirmation of Augustine that is related to eternal life. As we are in eternal life I would like to offer it to you:

> We shall rest and we shall see,
> We shall see and we shall know,
> We shall know and we shall love,

We shall love and we shall praise.
Behold our end, which is no end.
(*City of God*, chapter 35)

Let us not put off the fulfilment of this prayer to beyond the
grave but let us experience it now. In this way we shall learn that
we are already in the kingdom of God's love.

There is something wonderful about people who are at rest
in what they are doing, people who have let go of tension and
are at home in the world. This rest is a gift from God. It is the
devil who is restless. This rest reflects a life at peace with God.
This is a rest we can all enter each day. Do not put it off until
you die of exhaustion. Seek to learn of the rest that God gives
to his beloved. This rest is not doing nothing but rather working in harmony with God and his world: it is being in the kingdom of God.

In resting we have time to see more clearly. In resting we
become aware of what God has to offer to us. We see the world,
our God and ourselves in a better perspective. Resting helps us
to focus, to be more at home in God's world.

Resting helps us not only to focus on God but to know him.
'Be still and know that I am God.' Not only to see God at work
but to have a relationship with him. We need to move from just
saying 'I believe in God' to being able to say 'I know God – and
God knows me.' We must move from speaking about God to
speaking to God. God wants us to abide in him and know that
he abides in us. This knowing is not of the head but of the
heart. It will only grow well in a loving relationship, not one of
fear or servility.

To know God is to love him and to enjoy being with him.
When we find prayer boring or worship dull, we must remember the Almighty God can neither be boring nor dull. If we
cannot be bothered to pray it is because we have lost a vital

relationship with God or have not yet made it. The problem is not with God but with ourselves. If we feel God is far off it is because we have moved away or have not sought him. Each day make a homecoming and return to your God. This turning may begin with a confession of sin and penitence. It may be that you have wandered so far you are not sure where to turn. Know that as soon as you turn your Father comes to meet you. It is God who has called you and has been waiting for you. God welcomes you with open heart and open arms. Say to yourself, allowing each word to have impact:

> I will arise
> and go to my Father
> and say I have sinned before heaven and before you and
>     am not worthy . . .

Then let God accept you into his presence and enfold you in his love. Rest in the peace, in the power and in the presence of God who is Almighty. Let God renew, refresh and restore you. In the words of a hymn, let yourself be 'lost in wonder, love and praise'. A heart in tune with God is in his kingdom and in eternal life. Death has no dominion over this: 'Behold our end which is no end.'

### Exercises

1 Thoughts

> Think you the bargain's hard to have exchanged
> The transient for the eternal, to have sold
> Earth to buy heaven?
> (St Paulinus of Nola from Waddell, 1987, p. 30)

The one essential condition of human existence is that man should always be able to bow down to something

112

infinitely great. If men are deprived of the infinitely great they will not go on living and die of despair. The Infinite and the Eternal are as essential for man as the little planet on which he dwells.

(Fyodor Mikhailovich Dostoevsky, 1821–81)

2 Read the parable of the pearl of great price in Matthew 13.45–46.

**Pause, Presence, Picture, Ponder, Promise**

**Pause**   Stop all activity. Know he whom you seek is with you. Rest in the presence and in the power of God. You do not have to make efforts. You cannot make God come to you – he is with you always. Seek to rest in his presence as you would before a lake on a sunny day. Make sure each part of your body is free from tension. Let the peace of God flow into you. If the mind wanders say quietly:

> You Lord are in this place,
> your presence fills it,
> your presence is peace.

**Presence**   You do not have to imagine the Presence any more than you have to imagine the air about you. Know you are in God's presence, in his love and in his peace. Do not let other things take this away from you. Give your love to God and let him pour his love into your heart. 'Rejoice in the Lord.'

**Picture**   Pearls were very special in the ancient world and counted among the most precious possessions. The main sources for finding them were the shores of the Red Sea and the rivers of Britain. Pearls were traded for great prices. The merchant comes across a wonderful pearl in the market-place. The merchant has spent a lot of his time and energy in the search for precious pearls. This one is more than he could have hoped for – such beauty, such radiance. Picture him holding it, enjoying it, feeling he need not let this one slip from his grasp. He knows that he has come before something very special. If he is to have it he will have to trade – so what? He will give up all the lesser pearls to have this one. He knows he cannot just let this one go for there is not another like it. Picture him selling all that he has to gain this treasure.

**Ponder**   Think how the merchant spent a lot of time and energy seeking. He believed that what he sought was well worth having. If he did not seize the opportunity when it was offered him he might have lost it. If he did not give up other things for it now he might not get the same opportunity ever again. Jesus says the kingdom of heaven is like this. You may seek it but you also need to know when you have arrived. You need to discover that you are in the presence of God and in his kingdom. You should be able to delight in God and in the kingdom. This is beyond price. But are you too busy with other things to enjoy the heaven that is about you? Have you lost sight of the glory of God and the beauty of serving him? Think how well worthwhile it is to trade some temporal and passing goods for the eternal! Do not put things off – enjoy living in his kingdom today and knowing his love.

**Promise**   that you will spend some time each day delighting in the Presence and enjoying being a citizen of heaven.

3  Pray this and seek to show its reality in your life:

> Grant us, O Lord, to awake out of sleep,
> out of unbelief, little belief, dull belief,
> out of death into faith;
> and by hearing thy word,
> obeying thy will,
> doing thy works,
> to pass from darkness to light,
> from ignorance to knowledge,
> from blindness to sight;
> to move from repentance to pardon,
> from allegiance to love,
> from lethargy to power:
> And so declare the Father,
> and thee, Redeemer Lord,
> and the Holy and life-giving Spirit,
> one God, almighty, all-loving,
> world without end.
>                     (Milner-White, 1959, p. 102)

# Select Bibliography

Adam, D., 1985, *The Edge of Glory*, SPCK.

Ashwin, A., 1996, *The Book of a Thousand Prayers*, Marshall Pickering/ Zondervan.

Brother Lawrence, 1906, *The Practice of the Presence of God*, H. R. Allenson.

Carmichael, A., 1976, *Carmina Gadelica*, Vol. 3, Scottish University Press.

Davies, O. and Bowie, F., eds, 1995, *Celtic Christian Spirituality: An Anthology of Medieval and Modern Sources*, SPCK.

Dawkins, R., 1998, *Unweaving the Rainbow*, Allen Lane, Penguin Press.

de Chardin, P. Teilhard, 1975, *Le Milieu Divin,* Fontana.

Dickinson, E., 1970, *Complete Poems*, Faber & Faber.

Fabella, V., 1992, 'Symbols of John's resurrection scene: reflections on the garden and Mary Magdalene', in *Women of Courage: Asian Women Reading the Bible,* Lee Oo Chung et al., eds, Asian Women's Resource Centre for Culture and Theology.

Gardner, W. H. (ed), 1953, *Gerard Manley Hopkins: A Selection of His Poems and Prose*, Penguin.

Hardy, T., 1976, *The Complete Poems*, Papermac, Macmillan.

Hill, S., 1991, *Air and Angels*, Sinclair-Stevenson.

Holloway, R., 1984, *Paradoxes of Christian Faith and Life*, Mowbray.

Julian of Norwich, trans. members of the Julian Shrine, ed. R. Llewelyn, 1980, *Enfolded in Love*, Darton, Longman & Todd.

Lewis, C. Day, 1992, *The Complete Poems*, Sinclair-Stevenson.

Maclean, A., 1937, *Hebridean Altars*, Grant & Murray.

Meyer, K., trans., 1928, *Selections from Ancient Irish Poetry*, Constable.

# Select Bibliography

Milner-White, E., 1959, *My God, My Glory*, SPCK.

Oakley, M., ed., 2004, *John Donne, Verse and Prose*, SPCK.

Patterson-Smyth, J., 1913, *A People's Life of Christ*, Hodder & Stoughton.

*The SPCK Book of Christian Prayer*, 1995, SPCK.

Taylor, J. V., 1992, *The Christlike God*, SCM Press.

Thompson, F., 1910, *Selected Poems of Francis Thompson*, Methuen.

Toynbee, P., 1981, *End of a Journey*, Collins.

Vickers, S., 2000, *Miss Garnet's Angel*, HarperCollins.

Waddell, H., 1945, *Peter Abelard*, Constable.

Waddell, H., 1987, *The Desert Fathers*, Constable.

Watts, M., 1987, *Praying with St Augustine*, SPCK.

Williams, I., 1972, *The Beginnings of Welsh Poetry*, University of Wales Press.